The Food of Miami
Published by
Periplus Editions (HK) Ltd.
with editorial offices at
153 Milk Street
Boston, MA 02109
and
5 Little Road #08-01
Singapore 536983

ISBN: 962-593-231-3

Library of Congress Catalog Number: 98-45277

Credits
Endpapers: *South Beach Evening*, by Matthew Popielarz. Reproduced by permission of Matthew Popielarz.
Pages i, 6–9: images courtesy of the Charlton W. Tebeau Library of Florida History, the Historical Museum of Southern Florida. Reprinted by permission.
Page 15: *South Beach,* mixed media, by Alexander Chen, courtesy of Gallery Art. <www.artman.net>, tel: (800) 332-4278 © Alexander's World. Reprinted by permission.

First Edition
1 3 5 7 9 10 8 6 4 2
06 05 04 03 02 01 00 99
PRINTED IN SINGAPORE

Distributed by

USA
Tuttle Publishing
Distribution Center
Airport Industrial Park
364 Innovation Drive
North Clarendon, VT 05759-9436
Tel: (802) 773-8930
Tel: (800) 526-2778

Japan
Tuttle Publishing
RK Bldg. 2nd Floor 2-13-10 Shimo-Meguro,
Meguro-Ku Tokyo 153 0064
Tel: (03) 5437-0171
Fax: (03) 5437-0755

Canada
Raincoast Books
8680 Cambie Street
Vancouver, British Columbia
V6P 6M9
Tel: (604) 323-7100
Tel: (604) 323-2600

Asia Pacific
Berkeley Books Pte. Ltd.
5 Little Road #08-01
Singapore 536983
Tel: (65) 280-1330
Fax: (65) 280-6290

THE FOOD OF
MIAMI

Authentic Recipes from South Florida and the Keys

by Caroline Stuart

*With additional essays by Kendall Hamersly,
Howard Kleinberg, Nancy Klinginer, and Maricel Presilla*

*Featuring recipes from Caroline Stuart and
the following South Florida restaurants:*

Astor Place	*Norman's*
Blue Door	*Norma's On The Beach*
Cheeca Lodge	*Pacific Time*
Chef Allen's	*Sweet Donna's Country Store*
Deering Bay Yacht & Country Club	*Turnberry Isle Resort & Club*
Johnny V's Kitchen	*Twelve Twenty*
Louie's Backyard	*Two Chefs Cooking*
Mark's Las Olas	*Yuca*

*Photography by Jacob Termansen
Styling by Christina Ong*

PERIPLUS

Contents

Part One: Food in Miami

Everything under the sun

by Caroline Stuart

The food of Miami and the Keys is as surprising, varied, and colorful as its inhabitants. Cubans, Nicaraguans, Argentinians, and other Latin Americans; Haitians, Bahamians and Jamaicans; former slaves; transplants from other states—all of these came together in southern Florida to contribute to its delectable cuisine.

Miami's dazzling white beaches and seductive semitropical climate have been attracting large numbers of visitors and settlers from diverse cultures since its birth as a city just over 100 years ago. A decidedly Latin beat sets the rhythm for the collection of cities, neighborhoods, and islands known as the Greater Miami area. Latin American settlers happily found themselves in a familiar climate with familiar ingredients, and dishes such as black beans and rice, arroz con pollo (chicken with saffron rice), and garbanzo bean soup became the foods of Greater Miami.

New York transplants brought with them Jewish delicatessens that serve lox and bagels and traditional Kosher fare. Soul food can be found in homey barbecue joints that turn out racks of smoky pork ribs served with corn on the cob and collard greens. The region's early farmers contributed a blend of soul food and Southern country cooking that offers up dishes as popular as grits, hush pup-

pies, and deep-frys that today have made their way onto the menus of city restaurants; Bahamians added steamed pudding and conch (pronounced "konk") salad.

In South Beach, fashion shoots take advantage of light and location while residents and visitors crowd busy outdoor cafes. Restaurants serve grilled fish, tropical fruit salads, and sorbets of every hue. International cafes showcase ethnic specialties from around the world, and hot spots serve Asian-inspired dishes with a local flair.

In other parts of the city, home cooks scour the markets for familiar seafood and local specialties, such as conch for fritters and chowder and, in season, clawless Florida spiny lobster. Locally grown produce, including wild sour oranges, pineapples, coconuts, bananas, sugar cane, mangoes, guavas, papayas, and avocados, contributes to the cuisine.

South of Miami, the Florida Keys float like pearls, with Key West the last on the string. The Keys are a fishing enthusiast's paradise, where tarpon leap out of the water and the delicate yellowtail snapper is on everyone's list of favorites. Jimmy Buffett's song "Margaritaville" sets the tone for this laid-back area of Old Florida, the perfect place to savor the sunset along with the sweet-tart splendor of Key lime pie.

Page 2:
The 1937 Packard outside the Leslie Hotel recreates the atmosphere of one of Miami Beach's earlier high times.

A Culinary History of Miami

Fish in the summer, Yankees in the winter

by Caroline Stuart

The Timucua people inhabited the banks of the St. John's River during the sixteenth century. Occasionally chiefs and nobles would gather to discuss important issues, and during these meetings, the men would share an infusion of dried casina leaves. Only those who were able to consume the noxious liquid without becoming ill were deemed resiliant enough to defend the tribe.

Old-timers often declare that Miami and the Keys are not really a part of Florida anymore, but an extension of the Northeast and "the islands." Greater Miami encompasses a number of towns beneath its giant umbrella, but be it in Miami Beach, Coconut Grove, or Sweetwater, the flavor has gone global. You can find lox and bagels, Southern-fried chicken, Japanese sushi, Jamaican curried goat, and Cuban sandwiches within easy driving distance of one another. Grocery shopping, too, is international: an Asian market selling lemon grass may sit next door to a Latin *bodega* boasting an extensive se-

lection of tropical tubers—and both may be just down the street from a supermarket selling sour oranges for authentic Cuban marinades.

The culinary history of South Florida is one of immigration and adaptation. Even the area's Native Americans, the Seminoles, immigrated from other parts of North America. They may have been the ones who first slit open the base of the cabbage palm tree to harvest hearts of palm (the delicacy known to locals as "swamp cabbage"), which is frequently found on South Florida menus.

Spanish explorer Ponce de León reached Florida's shores in 1513, searching in vain for the legendary Fountain of Youth. He arrived on Easter Sunday, "Pascua Florida" (Feast of Flowers), and named the land *La Florida* in honor of the holiday. Other European explorers also trudged through Florida's swamps searching for gold, jewels, and natives for slave markets. But all early attempts to establish settlements failed.

The United States acquired Florida in 1821 and granted it statehood in 1845. From other states, a few hardy souls braved the mosquitoes and hostile natives to farm under the bright blue skies. These early farmers and their modern-day descendants are known as "Crackers," perhaps from the cracking sound of their cattle whips, perhaps from the cracking of corn to make grits.

Grits, made from dried, hulled corn that has been finely ground and cooked into a gruel, is eaten as a breakfast food or as a side dish with meat and fish. Grits and cornmeal remain staples of Southern cooking on Florida menus to this day. Cracker cooking is simple rustic food that can be as quirky as the characters who claim it. It incorporates Southern country cooking and soul food and includes oddities such as alligator, which is often served breaded and deep-fried, not unlike chicken nuggets.

Florida's isolation, alligators, and Indians made it a destination for escaping African slaves in the nineteenth century, who brought with them their native foodways to create what is known today as "soul food." Okra, black-eyed peas, fried chicken, and collard greens, as well as chitterlings, or "chitlins" (the small intestine of a hog) and cooter (soft-shelled freshwater turtle) are just a few of the "soul foods" that have become an integral part of the Florida menu.

Southern food, soul food, and Cracker cooking are today the culinary cousins that keep the old foodways alive.

The early settlers of the Keys—known as Conchs (pronounced "konks")—were Tories and seafarers from the Bahamas and New England. Their two foodways blended into one of the early fusion dishes that is now part of every Florida cook's repertoire: conch chowder. Conch is a mollusk that must be

This whimsical print from the late nineteenth century depicts a very real environmental hazard in the Everglades.

pounded to tenderness before being transformed into fritters, marinated salads or the ubiquitous creamy chowder made of conch stewed with tomatoes and hot spices. From the Keys also came the state dessert: Key lime pie. This creamy pie dates back to pre-refrigeration days in the 1850s, when canned condensed milk was introduced to the Keys. Florida was still mostly a wilderness when Northern Standard Oil magnate Henry Flagler extended his Florida East Coast Railroad to Miami in 1896. His trains carried carpetbaggers and speculators, the infirm seeking warm-weather cures and homesteaders. Flagler built lavish resort hotels to cater to wealthy Northerners.

The pace of development accelerated in the l920s, when a land boom made the area irresistible to Northerners lusting for fast money and seaside living. The boom inevitably went bust, but the lavish Mediterranean-style buildings it fostered left an enduring mark.

Miami kept its character as a resort town through the post-World War II era. Transplanted New Yorkers brought with them a taste for Jewish delicatessen items, such as corned beef sandwiches and lox and bagels, as well as an appreciation for the fine Florida seafood.

The arrival of Cuban exiles that began in 1959 sparked the transformation of Miami into a city of global flavors, and immigrants from all over Latin America joined Miami's great melting pot of flavors. Little Havana on Calle Ocho is the center of Cuban culture, but throughout the Greater Miami area, the population is nearly sixty percent Hispanic. You'll hear Spanish spoken as much as English on the streets, and it is easy to find and enjoy Cuban sandwiches (bread stuffed with pork, ham, salami, cheese and pickles that is usually pressed), *moros y cristianos* (black beans and rice), *picadillo* (ground meat, olives and capers), *tostones* (fried plantains), and *empanadas* (fried turnovers filled with meat, fish, poultry or fruit). Lit-

Miami is well-known for its cultural diversity and gustatory pleasures. In a photo from the Miami News, *a Rabbi enjoys donuts, alongside the creator of those delicious confections, in a bakery on Miami Beach.*

tle Haiti is where to find "Caribbean-style" chicken and plantains.

Here and there, especially in the laid-back Keys, word-of-mouth keeps track of the best barbecue joints and fish fry shacks, and old-timers may still be heard to say, "We live on fish in the summer and Yankees in the winter."

Time and again over the decades, Miami has been remade by waves of newcomers arriving from all over the world. But through it all, it has remained a mecca for visitors. Miami is second only to Disney World among Florida's many tourist attractions.

Today's sunseekers tend to be younger and more adventurous than in years past, more apt to order yellowtail snapper rather than sole, mango nectar instead of orange juice. Their worldly appreciation of fine cuisines has encouraged chefs in Miami and the Keys to make full use of the native abundance of tropical fruits, tubers, and seafood, transforming them into some of the most exciting fusion foods cooked in the United States today.

The melting pot that is Miami and the Keys continues to create a rich stew of cultures simmering in the tropical heat, a bold feast of international flavors constantly stirred by the hand of change.

The Florida Keys

Free spirit, good fishing, great food

by Nancy Klinginer

The great opportunity for deep-sea fishing and snorkeling off the only live coral reef in the United States is just one reason visitors flock to the Florida Keys, a chain of islands that stretches for one hundred miles off the southern tip of Florida.

Key West, the last link in the chain, is the most famous of the dozens of islands that make up the archipelago. In the Old Town section, wooden houses built by sailors and fishermen still stand defiantly after more than a century of hurricanes, termites, and neglect. These days, most of the houses are sparkling again, painted pale yellow or peach or blue, showing off their unique mix of New England ancestry and Bahamian openness.

Many Key Westers take their cue from the laid-back style of the local architecture—shirts and shorts are the town dress code, lawyers and doctors commute on old bicycles and your bartender is likely to have a Ph.D. as well as a ponytail. The old island's free spirit, good fishing, and warm winter weather attract throngs of tourists each winter. The numbers have grown in recent years, but pilgrims to Key West are nothing new. Writer Ernest Hemingway wintered here all through the 1930s, and Key West is the setting for his novel *To Have and Have Not*. His Whitehead Street home is a museum today and one of the island's most popular attractions.

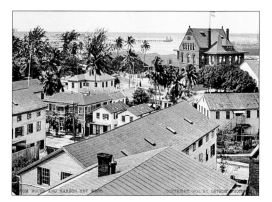

Tourism is just the latest in a varied line of livelihoods the Keys have drawn from the sea. Mostly, the waters have been generous, yielding fortunes in trade, fish and goods salvaged from ships that ran aground on the coral reef that parallels the islands.

The sea, however, also has punished the Keys. Hurricanes periodically roar across the Atlantic, blowing homes, businesses, and sometimes people out to sea. Even without storms, the subtropical climate, so soothing in winter, can be downright torturous during the still, simmering six-month summers. And isolation has at times brought poverty; the Great Depression was so dire in Key West that the federal government recommended closing the town and moving islanders. But the stub-

Custom House and harbor, Key West. The term "keys" comes from the Spanish word for "island," cayo.

born locals hung on, subsisting on a diet of "grits and grunts," corn porridge and a lowly local fish.

Settlement of the Keys began in earnest in the 1820s, when John Simonton bought Key West from Spaniard Juan Salas. It was a strategic location for the U.S. Navy, then chasing pirates from the region, just as their successors in the Navy, Coast Guard, and Customs Service chase drug smugglers today. It was also a natural trading outpost for ships carrying goods to and from the Eastern Seaboard, Gulf Coast, Caribbean, and South America.

Early settlers came from the Bahamas and New England. Made of coral rock, most of the islands have only a thin skin of soil for planting, so, like their fortunes, the settlers' food was provided by the sea. The catch includes conch, of course, plus turtle, crab, kingfish, lobster, and crawfish. Early Conchs (pronounced "konks"), as descendants of the first settlers proudly call themselves, supplemented scarce fresh produce with avocados, bananas, pineapples, coconuts, figs, dates, oranges, tamarinds, guavas, and mangoes from trees they planted on Key West.

As Cubans rebelled against Spanish colonial rule in the late 1800s, Key West experienced a large migration from its neighbor island across the Florida Straits. Entire cigar-factory operations were transplanted, igniting a cigar-making boom that briefly made Key West the nation's wealthiest city per capita.

Almost a century before the Cuban diaspora transformed Miami, Key West became a truly Cuban-American city, electing Cuban immigrants to the state legislature and the judiciary. With Cuban culture came Cuban food. Thick, sweet Cuban coffee in small cups is still a staple for many Key Westers, who call it *buche* (from *buchito,* "to swallow"). Ice cream is another island favorite. Decades before the current gourmet ice cream craze swept the United States, Keys aficionados used local fruit to churn out papaya, guava, mango, and coconut varieties.

The most famous food of the islands is Key lime pie. Also called Mexican lime, the small, thin-skinned Key lime is yellowish (if you're served a piece of green Key lime pie, you know it's a fake) and has a unique tartness and aroma. Its juice also is the primary component of a salty Key West marinade called Old Sour.

Today, the Keys boast a host of upscale restaurants, from which the chefs are maintaining tradition by taking their inspiration from the sea and from the Bahamian, Cuban, Anglo, and Caribbean cultures that have touched these small islands, which barely rise above the warm waters of the subtropical sea.

Miami Beach Heyday

Society and glamour give way to tourist trade—then return once again—
to Miami's ever-changing shore

by Howard Kleinberg

Miami Beach has had plenty of ups and downs over the years, but the 1950s and 1960s stand out as a magical time of glamour, excitement, and rapid expansion. Each year during those two decades, a spectacular new hotel would go up: the Algiers, the DiLido, the Fontainebleau, the Eden Roc, the Casablanca, the Americana, the Deauville, the Doral Beach. Miami Beach was in its heyday.

In its fancy hotels and nearby clubs, big-name entertainers drew throngs: Frank Sinatra crooned, Mitzi Gaynor danced, Alan King knocked them dead— even Sophie Tucker found a few bars to belt. Muhammed Ali liked to visit, as did Hollywood stars. The place was bursting at the seams as more and more visitors joined the fun.

It hadn't always been that way. Slow to evolve from its roots as a mangrove-laced sandbar, Miami Beach did not exist as a town until 1915. Put on the map by an early 1920s real estate boom, it was, until mid-century, a place to simply bask in the sun, ini-

tially for the nouveau riche of the Midwest, later for the Northeast's middle class.

An enduring facet of the city's character was forged in the 1930s, when a large Jewish population began emigrating to Miami Beach, chiefly from New York. Originally limited by restrictive developers and landlords to the southern end of the city, the new community ultimately moved north, bringing with them their corned beef and pastrami sandwiches, their sour pickles and Dr. Brown's Cel-Ray tonic. From Wolfie's down on 21st Street to the Rascal House up in Sunny Isles, residents and tourists alike seemed to take delight in being abused by Brooklyn-accented waitresses demanding, "Yeah, watcha want?" as they slammed pickle and sauerkraut bowls on the table.

During World War II, Miami Beach was introduced to middle America by an unlikely promoter—the U.S. military, which commandeered more than three hundred of its hotels and apartment houses as quarters for Army Air Corps cadets.

Thousands of young men (a full one-fifth of all who trained with the Army Air Corps) dropped their duffel bags in Miami Beach. Compared to pitching a tent somewhere in New Mexico, bunking in an oceanfront hotel must have been positively delightful. At war's end, many veterans, recalling their time in Miami Beach with fondness, boarded trains or planes with their families and headed back.

Tourists continued to swell Miami Beach's wintertime population, but by the 1950s their approach was less laid back. Now they came for much more than relaxation in the sun. They ate steaks and ribs at the Embers or up at Parham's, near Surfside. They dined regally at Gatti's on the bay side and lined up for hours for a meal at Joe's Stone Crab. They partied into the late hours, if not in the glitzy new hotels, then in the resort motels farther up the strip, where bawdy comics and brassy instrumentalists offered nighttime relief to sunburned parents who had finally gotten their kids off to bed.

Miami Beach lured visitors by perfecting the art of the "Come on down," first through a steady stream of oceanside cheesecake photos transmitted to the nation's mostly male newspaper photo editors, then through hugely popular radio and television programs. These included *Arthur Godfrey Time*, which began in the early 1950s, and occasional visits by *The Ed Sullivan Show*—one of them featuring

The Hotel Astor lobby has been restored to the height of Art Deco splendor. Today, chef Johnny Vinczencz lures a chic clientele with his "new American barbecue" cuisine at Astor Place, situated within the hotel.

the blockbuster first U.S. appearance of the Beatles in 1964. The long-running *Jackie Gleason Show*, which began broadcasting that year, warmed Miami Beach Chamber of Commerce hearts each week with its boastful opening, "From Miami Beach, the fun and sun capital of America."

A period of decay that began in the 1970s is nearly forgotten now, and the strip is again riding the waves of popularity. Today, Miami Beach is an upscale residential community with classic hotels and gourmet restaurants. Celebrities from many fields own homes here again, including Oprah Winfrey and singer Gloria Estefan. The Hollywood stars are back, as well, this time flocking to South Beach, along with supermodels, photographers, and fashion designers, echoing the glamour and excitement of glory days gone by.

Renovation and Rebirth on South Beach

Art Deco gets a facelift

by Howard Kleinberg

By night, Miami Beach's Art Deco district's trendy restaurants and glittering night spots attract the famous and the curious. By day, fashion photographers set up their cameras on the streets and angular models preen and pose. Photos of its sleek buildings adorn the covers of travel and fashion magazines worldwide, and the rich and famous from all over the world have made it one of their favorite gathering spots.

Yet not very long ago, South Beach, or SoBe—the section of Miami Beach south of 20th Street—was derelict: a collection of empty storefronts and small, frayed hotels where retirees sat on porches gazing out at Ocean Drive. It was seen as a district to be razed rather than raised. But no more.

The unrelenting passion of a group of preservation-minded fashion designers and the gamble of a few ambitious investors have succeeded in resurrecting South Beach and have helped to restore to Miami Beach some of the old glory it enjoyed during its heyday in the 1950s and 1960s.

Today's beautifully restored pastel-colored hotels had their origins as chalky white buildings designed by architects in the 1930s in styles variously labeled Zig Zag, Streamline, and Depression Moderne. The architects were working in the idiom of classic Art Deco, a school of design that combined the flowery forms of Art Nouveau and Egyptian motifs with the geometric patterns of Cubism to create a form that embodied the ideals of the New Machine Age.

Classical Art Deco took a sharp detour in Miami, however, when architects decided to incorporate whimsical tropical motifs into their designs: the concrete "eyebrows" that shade the windows of the Hotel Astor from the sun, the porthole-shaped windows of The Tides, the seahorse and tropical fish bas-relief that graces the facade of the Marlin, the octagonal concrete medallions that band the top of the Delano's sweeping entryway and repeated in its pastel terrazzo floor.

In the late 1960s, the term "Art Deco" came to encompass the vintage buildings of Ocean Drive, and in 1979, they became the first twentieth-century structures to be included in the National Register of Historic Places. Today, scant blocks away, lofty condominiums hover above the low-lying, restored structures of the Depression years.

This remarkable resurrection has drawn increasing numbers of rich and famous visitors from Europe, South America and the rest of the United States, including Hollywood, European, and Latin American stars, as well as the cream of the crop from the realm of international fashion. Once again, Miami Beach has arrived.

Opposite: South Beach, by Alexander Chen.

Cubans in Miami

At the forefront of a culinary revolution

by Maricel Presilla

They came by sea and by air in battered chartered planes and makeshift rafts and transformed Miami into a vibrant city with deep Latin roots. For Cubans are like the sturdy tubers at the core of their cuisine; they stay firmly in the ground and don't easily dissolve into their surroundings.

The first major wave of Cuban immigrants settled in the declining downtown area between Flagler and Eighth Streets, now known as Little Havana, in the early 1960s. Gradually, they moved north to Hialeah, west and south of Coral Gables, Key Biscayne, and other affluent areas, and, most recently, east of revitalized Miami Beach.

El Palacio de los Jugos (Palace of the Juice) is where Cuban Miami comes to shop for food.

South Florida's links to Cuba, however, go back as far as 1868, when immigrants and exiles transformed sleepy Key West into a prosperous Cuban enclave complete with cigar factories, social clubs, newspapers, restaurants, coffee shops, and schools. Key West also became a lively point of commercial exchange between Cuba and the United States. By the 1920s, entrepreneur Charles Brooks was shipping Cuban citrus fruits and avocados by boat to Key West and by train to points north. When a fierce hurricane destroyed the railway in 1935, Brooks planted citrus and avocados farther north, in Homestead, where his grandson, J. R., later founded Brooks Tropicals, Florida's largest shipper of tropical produce.

A quarter of a century later, Cuban immigrants planted fields of tropical root vegetables—starchy yuca, sweet boniato, and shaggy malanga—as well as plantains and tropical fruits, alongside the old groves in Homestead. The magnificent mamey sapote groves were protected by barbed wire and watchdogs, as if the leathery brown skin and sweet, salmon-colored flesh of the fruit enclosed gold nuggets instead of shiny black seeds.

Homero Capote, a farmer from central Cuba, is emblematic of the resilient wave of immigrants whose knowledge and toil fueled a culinary revolution that sustains Latin American cuisines in this country and provides the raw materials for some of our best Florida chefs. Capote began as a field worker but soon rented land of his own and experimented with the corn seeds and malanga corms his father sent. Over the years, Capote built up a thriving business of tropical tubers nurtured by hard work and commitment to his adopted land.

During the 1960s, Miami's once lonely and quiet downtown, its manicured sameness, also changed. The streets became crowded with small *bodegas* (grocery stores) and storefront Cuban restaurants serving fragrant black beans, hearty roast pork, and tender yuca doused in *mojo,* a tart, garlicky sauce of citrus juice and oil. Juice stands sold *batidos* (shakes made with dozens of exotic tropical fruits), and Cuban bakeries turned out guava pastries and elaborately decorated cakes for the lavish *fiestas de quince,* with which Cuban families celebrate their daughters' fifteenth birthdays.

On weekends, Cuban families flocked to Key Biscayne with makeshift kitchens in tow. They filled the peaceful, tree-lined beach at Cape Florida with Latin radio music and fast-paced Spanish dialog. While the children swam, parents and grandparents cooked meals under the pine trees, and the tempting aroma of Cuban barbecue and rice and beans warmed the ancient stones of the lighthouse.

At the time, two kinds of restaurants catered to the burgeoning Cuban population: large, ornate Spanish establishments that appealed to their strong Spanish roots and the Mediterranean elements of their cuisine, and small cafeterias. The cafeterias were oases where people went late at night to eat Cuban sandwiches with *café con leche* (coffee with lots of milk) or during the day to meet and talk over sips of strong coffee from tiny paper cups.

Miami Cubans are like the coffee they drink: bittersweet, intense, and passionate, embracing their new home with the same ferocity with which they cherish their native Cuba. It is this paradoxical longing for what was lost and attachment to what is new that has transformed Miami into a hybrid Cuban city where even the old men playing dominoes on Eighth Street (*Calle Ocho*), nostalgic for Cuba, are among the most devoted of Miamians.

Each new wave of immigrants has refreshed the "Cubanness" lost by the previous, more assimilated groups. A virtual tidal wave of immigrants washed over South Florida in 1980, when Castro released 125,000 Cubans. In the years that followed, open-air markets that resembled chunks of Cuba—with pigs roasting close to the sidewalk, outdoor fruit stands, and people sitting down on wooden stools to drink coconut juice— sprouted in Miami. Once the most popular of

There are several interesting cafes in and around Española Way serving a variety of Cuban staples.

Though Cuban coffee may look like espresso, don't be fooled by apperances. It is even thicker and stronger.

For Cubans and other Latin Americans, the road to Miami was built of shattered dreams and the mortar of new hope. At the road's end sits a great pot in which the flavors of all of Latin America simmer and beckon. You can sample Salvadoran *pupusas* (stuffed tortillas), Argentinian *churrasco* (grilled meat), and Nicaraguan *tres leches* ("three milks" cake). The town of Sweetwater has become the heart of the Nicaraguan community, where you can enjoy desserts in informal cafeterias and small bakeries and flavorful meats at elegant steak houses. Adding to the traditional bastions of Cuban fare, such as Versailles and La Carreta on Eighth Street, are newer, upscale restaurants, including Yuca and Victor's Cafe, offering an inventive, hybrid cuisine.

Part of the ongoing cultural replenishment of Miami is the merging of food and music. People go to restaurants where they can also enjoy shows by performers newly arrived from Cuba. This is the kind of lively night life for which Havana was once famous.

Every year before Lent, Miami explodes into the "Calle Ocho Festival," a huge carnival sponsored by the Kiwanis Club of Little Havana to celebrate a community that has come of age. Its core is on Calle Ocho, where the first Cuban immigrants settled and where every block is crowded with kiosks, the smell of Cuban *tamales*, roast pork and black beans and rice mingling with that of Colombian *arepas* (corn patties) and Peruvian *anticuchos* (skewered beef heart). And then there is the music. Rhythmic and infectious, it captures the essence of those who move easily between two worlds and dance to one celebratory Miami beat.

these markets, El Palacio de los Jugos, is now a must-see for any food writer and tourist visiting the area.

Drawn by the success of the Cubans, many other Latin Americans began settling in the region. Miami became the emotional and economic capital of the Latin American world, attracting many of its movie and television stars and pop singers. Today, 1.1 million, or nearly 60 percent, of metropolitan Miami's 2 million residents are Latin-American, about half of them Cuban. The Cuban population continues to grow as Cubans living elsewhere in the United States fulfill what seems to be their destiny: to end their days in Miami.

Dining Out in Miami

Order a big dish of ropa vieja—and be sure to wear your best threads

by Kendall Hamersly

South Florida is a fusion of cultures, and South Florida dining is a fusion of cuisines—dishes from around the globe coming together in the same neighborhood, in the same restaurant, on the same plate. If you want to stamp a name on it, you can call it New Florida, New World, or Floribbean, but it is not so easily categorized.

The top of the dining pyramid is the domain of the Mango Gang, a loose group of innovators who invented New Florida cuisine, a casual fusion of the Caribbean, Latin America, Asia, and Middle America. The big three are Allen Susser (of the elegant **Chef Allen's** in Aventura), rising national star Norman Van Aken (**Norman's** in Coral Gables) and Mark Militello (whose flagship **Mark's Place** has closed, but who now has the stunning and popular **Mark's Las Olas** in nearby Fort Lauderdale). These are the proving grounds and showcases for the best and most adventurous of the New Florida cuisine.

Yet the bottom of the pyramid, restaurants where you can dine for ten dollars or so, offers culinary adventures, as well. Little Havana, the neighborhood just west of downtown Miami, has the greatest concentration of Cuban restaurants in the United States, mostly rock-bottom budget places where you can gorge yourself on palomilla steak (sirloin marinated in garlic and lime juice, pounded thin and quickly fried), sweet fried plantains, and black beans and rice. A shining example (literally; just wait until you see the mirrors and chandeliers) is **Versailles**, where the tuxedoed wait staff applies the highest standards of service to the delivery of your six-dollar platter of *ropa vieja* (shredded beef in a savory tomato sauce).

Coral Gables' reputation for fine dining is the best in metropolitan Miami. In the heart of the Gables, a mix of charming Mediterranean architecture and futuristic office buildings, are dozens of superbly run restaurants with impeccable service and a dressy feel. In addition to Norman's, highlights include **Giacosa**, perhaps the area's best Italian restaurant, and **The Heights**, a spinoff of **Pacific Time**, Jonathan Eismann's bastion of Asian Rim

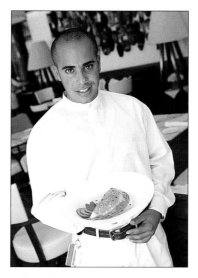

Waiter from the Blue Door ready to serve.

A typical South Beach restaurant— very fun and noisy.

Opposite: Although neons and pastels are the dominant colors in South Beach architecture, The Tides breakfast atmosphere is enhanced by the facade's soothing off-white.

cooking in South Beach. Where Pacific Time has a light, fish-oriented menu, The Heights takes a heartier, more Middle American approach.

If it's down-home cooking you're looking for, one of the Gables' most popular eateries is the **Biscayne Miracle Mile**, a cafeteria specializing in Southern soul food. Put the Mile's 85-cent collard greens up against most $7.95 salads in a blind taste test, and you've saved yourself seven dollars and change. Nuevo Cuban cuisine has a major outpost in the Gables, though it's not a nuevo place: **Victor's Cafe**,

founded in New York two decades ago and imported south, features dishes like red snapper in crunchy green plantain crust.

In nearby South Miami, **Two Chefs Cooking**'s Jan Jorgensen and Soren Brendahl apply Mediterranean touches to hearty fare that one appreciative critic described as "nouvelle bistro." In Coconut Grove, **The Grand Café** at the Grand Bay Hotel dazzles visiting celebrities with its upscale menu.

The seafood hot spot of the moment in the Coral Gables-South Miami area is **Red Fish Grill**, a one-time beach house in Matheson Hammock Park on tree-lined Old Cutler Road. On a cool spring evening, you'll think you've died and gone to Hemingway as you dine outside on delicate, pan-seared sea bass. Farther down Old Cutler, at the private **Deering Bay Yacht & Country Club**, fish with tropical flourishes star on chef Paul Gjertson's menu. Along U.S. Route 1, you'll find the area's best family fish house, the **Captain's Tavern**, with an ideal mix of both simple fried fish and designer seafood. Also on U.S. Route 1, near the University of Miami, is the southern branch of downtown Miami's **Fishbone Grille**, where Chef David Bracha does a delectable Bahamian-style whole yellowtail with pigeon peas, rice and Scotch bonnet vinaigrette.

South Florida's best seafood is found, not surprisingly, in the Keys. Upper Matecumbe Key, which includes Islamorada and is roughly ninety miles south of downtown Miami, has nearly thirty restaurants in its three-mile span. At the picturesque **Morada Bay**, chef Alex Kaulbach mixes tuna steak with black beans and pineapple in Thai peanut sauce. At **Atlantic's Edge**, chef Dawn

Astor Place, the bistro-style restaurant at the Hotel Astor.

Today, the region's emerging fine-dining destination is affluent Aventura, in the far northeast corner of Dade County. Aventura is home to **Fish**, which features a 20,000 Leagues atmosphere, a bustling raw bar, and such elegant entrées as grouper with creamy leeks, French lentils, and wild mushrooms. And at the private **Turnberry Isle Resort & Club**, chef Todd Weisz is serving the upscale clientele an upscale take on Floribbean.

Flash south along the coast and east across Biscayne Bay to South Beach, or SoBe, the so-called American Riviera, where the Art Deco revival fostered a revolution in tourism, nightlife, and dining. The Beach scene has a reputation for high prices and indifferent service, and some of that is deserved, but there's a high degree of glamour at work here, too. Take the **Blue Door** restaurant at The Delano, a blindingly white hotel in northern South Beach. The restaurant is a bustling, chaotic, super-crowded, see-and-be-seen spot—you might even end up sitting ten feet from Calvin Klein or Madonna. The Delano has competition in the swank hotel department in The National, its neighbor to the south on suddenly exploding Collins Avenue. Refurbished and reopened to much fanfare in 1997, The National is home to the **Oval Room**, featuring one of the city's most sophisticated menus. Ocean Drive, ground zero for the SoBe revolution, is more oriented toward fun than food these days, with the exception of chef Christophe Gerard's elegant **Twelve Twenty** at The Tides Hotel. Two blocks inland on Washington Avenue, chef Johnny Vinczencz's **Astor Place** may offer the best combination of food and service on the Beach, with a menu that's all about

Sieber bakes dolphin in phyllo dough with spinach and balsamic glaze and cooks spicy orange shrimp in dark rum. For the seafood purist, the **Islamorada Fish Co.** offers up standards such as conch chowder, crab fritters and the absolute freshest of fish, served in a basket with coleslaw and french-fries, for less than ten dollars. At **Louie's Backyard** in Key West, chef Doug Shook is following in the illustrious footsteps of Norman Van Aken, who brought Louie's to the forefront of the then-nascent Keys fine-dining scene in the 1980s.

fusion, from a fantastic Caribbean seafood soup to a cold sushi-plate entrée. You can also catch his food at his nearby casual diner, **Johnny V's Kitchen**. Farther south on Washington is **China Grill**, an outpost of the wildly popular New York restaurant. The food is pan-Asian, excellent and expensive, and the wait can be forty-five minutes or more on a weekend, even with a reservation.

The crowds are just as heavy a few blocks east at **Nemo**, the Schwartz-Chefetz team's flagship restaurant, where Schwartz matches fish with exotic greens and adds Vietnamese spice to an excellent beef tenderloin. Across the street is their budget house, the **Big Pink**, where the camp factor is so high that you can get a bona fide TV dinner on a compartmentalized tray. The food is homemade, though, and good.

North of Fifth Street, Washington Avenue is evolving into a strand of nightclubs and clothing stores, but it is still home to the Beach's best Italian restaurant, **Osteria del Teatro**. By and large, Beach sophisticates have moved north to the newly renovated Lincoln Road, a pedestrian mall that spans the island from ocean nearly to bay. Much of the eating there is done outdoors, and on weekend nights during the season, the walkways are packed.

Outstanding restaurants abound, not all of them expensive, and fans of Italian are especially well rewarded. **Rosinella's**, a tiny trattoria on the East End, features excellent homemade pastas, sauces and soups, with a full-meal ticket of about twenty dollars. **Trattoria da Leo**, farther west, has a similar menu and a surprisingly sophisticated decor and clientele (don't miss the world's best house salad).

The British invasion of Lincoln Road, begun by Michael Caine with his **South Beach Brasserie**, continues with **Balan's**, opened by a London-based group with a flair for combining hip sophistication with fine Thai-, Chilean-, and Moroccan-influenced food at a budget price. Fiery Jamaican food, cooled a bit to stateside tastes, is on display at **Norma's On The Beach**, where chef Cindy Hutson flies in many ingredients from the island. Cuban cuisine at its most sophisticated is served at **Yuca**, on the mall neighboring the Lincoln Theatre, where the New World Symphony performs. When the orchestra plays early on a Saturday evening, you can sit outside, sip cafe con leche, and listen in as the concert is broadcast onto the mall.

A symphony of flavors? Or better yet, call it a fusion. Bravo!

Bigfish Mayaimi, located on the Miami River, purveys an eclectic mix of seafood cuisine and scintillating artwork.

Part Two: The Miami Kitchen

With simple equipment, easy techniques, and a palette of local and international flavors, the food of South Florida comes dazzlingly alive

For cooking the food of Miami and the Keys the equipment isn't elaborate and typical kitchens contain just about everything necessary. Stockpots, saucepans, and sauté pans are essential. For frying, a deep fryer is useful, but a deep frying pan or heavy saucepan will suffice.

For cracking hard lobster shells and crab claws, a long-handled pounder, or "basher," is useful. Also useful are lobster crackers that are 6 to 8 inches long and hinged. Another handy utensil is the lobster pick—a long, slim fork with two short angled prongs for getting bits of luscious crab or lobster meat from hard-to-reach areas.

Citrus juice is used a good deal in Miami cooking, so an electric juicer, a long-handled wooden reamer or a citrus press for smaller fruit segments will make things easier. To juice the fruit without cutting the flesh, spear one end of a lemon or lime with a dinner fork, working the tines in and out to crush the inside pulp of the fruit. Over a small bowl, hold the handle of the fork in one hand and squeeze the fruit with the other to extract the juice.

Floridians do a lot of outdoor cooking over charcoal or a charcoal grill, although in most cases a broiler can be substituted. Traditional grill utensils are long-handled tongs, forks, spatulas for turning food on the grill, a basting brush and a stiff wire brush for cleaning the grill. Skewers, both metal and wooden, are sold for threading food so it will hold its shape and won't fall through the grill rack while cooking.

The food of Miami and the Keys also uses many familiar ingredients, as well as a number of less well-known products of international heritage. Many of these are readily available; for source and shopping information call 1-800-526-2778.

ANNATTO: This somewhat musky-flavored, rusty-red spice, also known as achiote, lends a yellow color and a subtle flavor to Caribbean foods. Often, the whole seeds are used to flavor cooking oils. In its powdered form, it is called **bijol**. Many people call annatto the "poor man's saffron," but its earthy flavor is distinctively different. You'll find it in markets that carry Latin American products.

BANANA and **BANANA LEAF**: Many choices of banana will tempt you in markets, from small finger bananas to the ubiquitous Cavandish. Banana leaves, available in some Latin American markets, are used to wrap food and to line the oven when baking Cuban bread. Parchment paper and aluminum foil may be substituted, but the flavor of the bananas will be missing.

Calabaza

Chayote

Chorizo

Guava

CALABAZA: The West Indian pumpkin, or Cuban squash, is a hard-shelled squash with dense, yellow flesh and a flavor similar to Hubbard or butternut squash. It can be round or pear-shaped with orange, green or striped skin. Because it can grow so large, it is often sold in plastic-wrapped chunks. Substitute North American pumpkin or winter squash.

CHAYOTE: This pale green, tropical squash has a thick, edible skin and a single seed. The flesh has a crisp texture and is more delicate in flavor than the familiar summer squash. This Central American native goes by many names, including mirliton, christophene, and vegetable pear.

CHORIZO: This highly seasoned, coarsely ground, spicy pork sausage is used in Spanish, Mexican, and Caribbean cooking. It is available in Latin American markets. Substitute any spicy pork sausage.

CITRUS: You'll find all manner of citrus fruits thriving in the state, one of the world's largest producers. It is also popular as backyard fruit. The most familiar are the orange, grapefruit, lime, lemon, and tangerine, but more exotic varieties are grown, including the kumquat, tangelo, pomelo, and calamondins. Some varieties of the familiar grapefruit and oranges are never shipped outside the area and are worth sampling if you are visiting. Choose citrus by weight, not color; the heavier fruits will contain more juice.

COCONUT: The coconut is the large, hairy fruit of the coconut palm tree. The flesh lining the inside shell is white. When choosing one, shake it and be sure there is liquid inside. Coconut milk is made by steeping the sweet white meat with water and then straining it. Canned coconut milk is readily available and may be substituted.

CONCH (pronounced "konk"): This large mollusk has a shell that is sometimes 9 to 12 inches in diameter. The beautiful shell is spiral shaped with yellow shading to pink inside and the one that tourists favor as a souvenir. It has been known to be used by fishermen as a trumpet to announce an incoming catch, and when held to the ear, it is said that one can hear the ocean. The flesh inside the shell is considered a delicacy. It must be tenderized before using by pounding with a mallet. It often is made into fritters, chowders or stews. The term "conch" also refers to someone who was born and raised in the Florida Keys. Substitute abalone.

GRITS: A specialty of the South, grits is made from finely ground, dried hulled corn kernels. Grits is boiled to make a thickened gruel similar to polenta (but coarser in texture) and served as either a breakfast food or a side dish.

GUAVA: The guava is a round fruit, 2 to 6 inches in diameter, with thick, edible skin, which may be greenish white, yellow or red when the fruit is ripe. It contains small seeds embedded in a soft, sweet, white, pale yellow or pink pulp. The gritty seeds are often removed by passing the flesh through a sieve. Some compare the flavor of the fruit to strawberries. It can be eaten raw or cooked and is mostly used in jelly-making and paste. Guavas are also used as a base for glazes and custards. They are available fresh and sold canned as guava paste, stewed guava shells and guava jelly. When cooking, they have a distinctive aroma that some find unappealing.

HEART OF PALM: Floridians call this delicacy "swamp cabbage." It is the tender heart of the sabal palm and can be eaten raw or cooked, in salads, or as a vegetable. The tree must be destroyed to obtain the heart from the center, and state requirements protect the trees from harvest by issuing permits. After the palm is cut down, the fibrous layers of sheathing are cut and peeled off revealing the delicate heart. When fresh, the white flesh is crunchy and mild tasting; the canned variety has a softer consistency. Fresh swamp cabbage can be found in some farm stands, and it is available canned in supermarkets.

KEY LIME: Residents of the Keys take great pride in their unique Key limes, grown primarily in the Florida Keys. It is smaller than the familiar Persian lime and has a greenish yellow skin. The juice is used when making the most famous Key lime pie. It is known as the Mexican, West Indies or true lime. Substitute one regular (Persian) lime for every three Key limes called for in a recipe.

LEMON GRASS: This fragrant lemon-scented grass looks like a miniature leek and is used whole or pounded as part of a spice mix in Asian-inspired dishes. When pounding lemon grass, slice off the root end and peel off several tough outer leaves. Use only the tender bottom (about 4 inches). Slice before pounding or blending.

LITCHI: An attractive, small, oval-shaped fruit with a hard red shell and white juicy flesh surrounding a single large seed. Buy them fresh or canned. Also known as litchee or lychee.

MANGO: This fruit ranks among the favorites of Floridians. It is green when unripe and in varying colors from green to rose red when ripe. The flesh is pale to deep yellow and the sweet flesh is used in desserts, drinks and ice cream. To remove the pulp, peel and cut the fruit away from the fibrous seed. Unripe mango is used for chutneys and relishes.

OLD BAY SEASONING: Old Bay Seasoning is the proprietary name of a spice blend that is often used to season shellfish and poultry. It is made from celery salt, dry mustard, paprika and other flavorings.

PAPAYA: Also known as "paw-paw," this melon-like fruit has a smooth, thin skin in colors that range from deep orange to green. The smooth flesh is white before maturity, turning to a rich yellow-pink to yellow-orange as the fruit ripens. It is often eaten "on the half shell" with a squeeze of lime over it and is used in sauces, preserves, desserts and salads. The unripe fruit is also prepared as a vegetable and used to make chutney and relishes. The small, spicy seeds are round, grayish black and edible; they are often used as a garnish.

PASSION FRUIT: Most commonly golf ball–sized and purple-brown with a wrinkled shell-like covering, the passionfruit contains yellow pulp that tastes like a combination of lemon, pineapple and guava. The fruit is ripe when you can hear liquid sloshing inside the skin when you shake the fruit.

PLANTAIN: Closely related to bananas, these starchy vegetables are never eaten raw but are

Hearts of Palm

Key Limes

Papaya

Passion Fruit

Plantains

Starfruit

Stone Crab

Yuca

used in cooking at every stage from green to dead-ripe. The flavor is mild, and they are often served instead of potatoes. Plantains will ripen at room temperature, taking one week to go from green to yellow-brown (semi-ripe) and another week or two to become black and fully ripe.

SOUR ORANGE: The sour orange, also called the bitter orange or Seville orange, is reputed to have been introduced to Florida by Spanish explorers and their seeds discarded by roaming Native Americans, which explains why sour oranges grow wild in the state. They can also be found in farm stands and some supermarkets. Sour oranges look like regular oranges but the flesh is sour. They are used for marinades or made into marmalade. A mixture of lemon and lime, with a touch of sweet orange juice, makes a barely acceptable substitute.

SPINY LOBSTER: The Florida lobster has the meat in the tail and lacks the large front pincer claws of its New England relative. The meat, usually sold as a frozen tail, is snow-white and sweet. . Because of its scarcity, there is a spiny lobster season, and the numbers and size are restricted. Substitute Maine lobster. Florida lobster is the same crustacean that is known as Rock lobster, and as *langouste* in France and *aragosta* in Italy.

STAR FRUIT: This is a delightful translucent yellow or golden orange tropical fruit with a thin, waxy edible rind and a crisp, juicy, yellow interior. It is oval shaped with prominent ribs that run the length; when sliced, the cross-sections look like stars. It is eaten raw. Also called carambola.

STONE CRAB: Stone crabs are a cherished specialty in South Florida and the Keys where they seem to thrive. They have a dense shell and black-tipped claws, the only part of the crab that is actually served. They may only be caught from mid-October to mid-May, and there are size regulations imposed by the state. The law also specifies that only the larger of the crab's two claws may be harvested, and that the live crab must be returned to the sea to grow a new claw. Substitute any other crabmeat.

TAMARIND: The pod of the tamarind tree contains seeds covered by fleshy pulp, which add a fruity sourness to many dishes inspired by Asian and Caribbean cuisine. Tamarind is often sold in blocks of pulp, which contain seeds and fibers. The pulp is usually soaked in liquid, then strained before using. Canned tamarind liquid is sometimes available where Indian foods are sold.

YUCA: These tropical tubers, which also go by the names of cassava and manioc, are at least 2 inches in diameter and about 8 to 10 inches long. They have a brown, bark-like skin with a hard, starchy, white flesh. There are two varieties of yuca, sweet and bitter. Bitter yuca can be poisonous until cooked. It is said that the Arawak Indians ate it raw to commit suicide to escape the wrath of intruding Spanish troops. It is usually cooked and eaten in fritters and stews, or boiled and served as a starchy vegetable. Found in grocery stores that cater to a Hispanic clientele; substitute potatoes or yams if necessary.

Part Three: The Recipes
Basic Recipes

Adobo Seasoning
Carmen González

2 garlic cloves, minced
3$^{1}/_{4}$ teaspoons salt
2 teaspoons extra-virgin olive oil
1 teaspoon white vinegar

Combine all of the ingredients and mix well.

Mojo Marinade
Norman Van Aken, Norman's

6 garlic cloves, minced
1 Scotch bonnet pepper (or other hot fresh
   pepper), seeded
$^{1}/_{2}$ teaspoon salt
2 teaspoons cumin seeds, toasted
1 cup pure olive oil
2$^{1}/_{2}$ tablespoons orange juice
2$^{1}/_{2}$ tablespoons lime juice
2 teaspoons Spanish sherry vinegar
Salt and pepper

Mash the garlic, hot pepper, salt, and cumin seeds together in a blender or mortar and pestle until fairly smooth. Scrape into a bowl and set aside. In a sauté pan, heat the olive oil until fairly hot and pour it over the garlic mixture. Let it stand for 10 minutes. Whisk in the citrus juices and the vinegar. Season with salt and pepper to taste. Allow to cool before pouring over meat. Yields about 1$^{1}/_{3}$ cups.

Sofrito
Carmen González

2 Spanish onions, peeled and quartered
2 Cubanelle peppers, seeded
2 garlic cloves, peeled
1 cup cilantro leaves
3 tablespoons green olives stuffed with pimento

Combine all of the ingredients in a blender or food processor and puree.

Seven-Minute Frosting

1$^{1}/_{2}$ cups sugar
2 egg whites
$^{1}/_{4}$ teaspoon cream of tartar
5 tablespoons cold water
1 teaspoon light corn syrup
1 teaspoon coconut extract

Combine all of the ingredients in the top half of a double boiler. Place over boiling water and mix with an electric mixer for 7 minutes or until the frosting increases in volume and holds stiff peaks. Remove from the heat. Continue to mix at high speed until fluffy and of a spreadable consistency, about 10 minutes. Immediately frost the cake. Yields enough frosting for one 9-inch, 3-layer cake.

*Jamaican-Spiced
Grilled Pork
(opposite)*

STONE CRAB CLAWS & GOLDEN CRAB CAKES

STONE CRAB CLAWS

Stone crab claws are a South Florida seasonal specialty. Usually they are eaten cold. Some dip the crabmeat into melted butter, but the most popular sauce served with them is a mustard sauce. The claws are always sold pre-cooked.

Mustard Sauce
   1 cup mayonnaise
   1 tablespoon dry mustard
   2 teaspoons Worcestershire sauce
   1 teaspoon steak sauce
   2 tablespoons light cream
   $^1/_8$ teaspoon salt

   2 pounds stone crab claws, cooked, chilled, and cracked

Mix all the sauce ingredients, except the cream, in a mixer or blender.

Gradually add the cream and beat at slow speed until it thickens. Cover with plastic wrap and chill until ready to use.

To serve, divide the stone crab claws among 4 to 6 large dinner plates and serve the mustard sauce in a bowl. Serves 4 to 6.

GOLDEN CRAB CAKES

These crab cakes are fabulous. The sweet meat of the deepwater golden crab is accentuated in these cakes, which contain mostly crabmeat and very lit-tle filler. They freeze well. Defrost and pan-fry just before serving. If you like, serve with the **Key Lime Mustard Sauce** (page 38).

   1 pound golden crabmeat (or substitute other crabmeat)
   1 egg yolk, beaten
   3 scallions, thinly sliced
   $^1/_3$ cup finely chopped Italian parsley
   1 tablespoon mayonnaise
   1 tablespoon Dijon-style mustard
   1 tablespoon fresh lemon juice
   Worcestershire sauce to taste
   Salt and freshly ground black pepper to taste
   $^1/_3$ loaf white bread (about 6 slices), crusts removed
   Vegetable oil for frying

Squeeze the excess water from the crabmeat and remove any shells or cartilage. In a mixing bowl, combine the crabmeat and all of the remaining ingredients, except the bread and oil. Mix well to combine and adjust the seasoning. Put the bread into a blender or food processor and process into fine crumbs. Add the crumbs to the crab mixture and mix until the bread is well coated. Form the crab cakes and chill well.

Pan-fry the cakes over medium-high heat in 1 inch of oil until nicely browned, about 5 minutes per side. Serve hot. Yields 6 to 7 crab cakes.

SPICY SHRIMP WITH RUM-MARINATED PINEAPPLE

Doug Shook, Louie's Backyard

Shrimp is very popular in South Florida, and whether served as an appetizer or as party fare, you can be sure that this dish will be a favorite. Both the shrimp and the spicy marinade can be made ahead of time. Add the Chinese chili paste gradually to spice it to taste.

The rum-marinated pineapple makes a refreshing contrast to the shrimp's sharp Asian seasonings. Golden pineapple is an especially flavorful variety, but any type of pineapple may be substituted.

Shrimp

- 1 onion, roughly chopped
- 4 celery ribs, roughly chopped
- 2 carrots, sliced
- 2 bay leaves
- 1 tablespoon black peppercorns
- 2 pounds shrimp (16 to 20 count), unpeeled

Spicy Marinade

- 3 tablespoons Chinese chili paste with garlic
- 3 tablespoons brown sugar
- 3 tablespoons rice vinegar
- 3 tablespoons sesame oil
- 2 teaspoons soy sauce
- 2 teaspoons white sesame seeds, toasted
- 2 teaspoons black sesame seeds, toasted
- $1/2$ cup diced green or red bell pepper
- 3 tablespoons chopped cilantro

Rum-Marinated Pineapple

- 2 tablespoons fresh lime juice
- 2 tablespoons fresh lemon juice
- 2 tablespoons fresh orange juice
- 2 tablespoons dark rum
- 2 tablespoons falernum (a West Indian syrup, available in liquor stores)
- $1/2$ teaspoon freshly grated nutmeg
- 1 pineapple (golden variety recommended)

For the **shrimp**, combine all the ingredients, except the shrimp in a large pot with 4 quarts of water. Bring to a boil and cook for 10 minutes. Add the shrimp and cook until pink and just cooked through, about 5 minutes. Drain the shrimp, discarding the broth, and refrigerate until cool. Peel and devein the shrimp, leaving the tails intact.

Combine all the **marinade** ingredients in a non-reactive bowl, add the shrimp, cover and marinate.

For the **pineapple**, mix the citrus juices with the rum, falernum, and nutmeg. Trim the pineapple and cut each quarter into 4 to 6 wedges. Toss with the rum mixture an hour before serving and refrigerate.

To serve, mound the shrimp in the center of a bowl. Drain the pineapple, and arrange it around the shrimp. Serves 4 to 6.

Helpful hint: For a more festive dish, cut the outside edge of each pineapple wedge in a zigzag design.

SEAFOOD MARGARITA

Johnny Vinczencz, Astor Place, Johnny V's Kitchen

Smoked Fish Dip

- 10 ounces smoked dolphinfish (mahimahi) or other white, flaky smoked fish
- 5 ounces cream cheese
- 1 chipotle pepper
- 1 stalk of celery
- $\frac{1}{2}$ small white onion
- Salt and pepper to taste

Shrimp Cocktail

- 12 extra-large (15 per pound) shrimp
- 1 carrot, cut in 1-inch rounds
- 1 stalk celery, cut in 1-inch rounds
- $\frac{1}{2}$ Spanish onion, cut in 1-inch slices

Three-Herb Pesto

- $\frac{1}{3}$ cup basil
- 1 tablespoon fresh thyme leaves
- $\frac{1}{4}$ cup cilantro leaves
- $\frac{3}{4}$ cup vegetable oil
- $\frac{1}{4}$ teaspoon black pepper

Chipotle Lime Vinaigrette

- $\frac{1}{4}$ cup cilantro leaves
- 1 chipotle pepper
- 1 garlic clove
- Juice of 2 limes
- $\frac{3}{4}$ cup vegetable oil
- 2 tablespoons honey
- $\frac{1}{4}$ cup red wine vinegar
- $\frac{1}{2}$ teaspoon black pepper
- $\frac{1}{2}$ teaspoon salt

- 2 cooked Maine lobster tails, cut in half
- 4 cooked Maine lobster claws, removed from the shell
- 4 ounces king crabmeat
- Red chili powder
- 2 cups baby salad greens or mesclun
- 4 potato crackers (page 136)
- 8 chive sprigs for garnish
- Garnish: Baby frisée or curly endive

Combine the **fish dip** ingredients, except the salt and pepper, in a food processor and process until smooth. Season to taste with salt and pepper.

Skewer the **shrimp** lengthwise on 12 bamboo skewers to prevent curling during cooking. Bring 4 cups water and the vegetables to a boil in a large saucepan. Add the shrimp, cook for 4 minutes, then remove and chill in ice water.

To make the **pesto**, put all of the ingredients in a blender and process until smooth. Rub the mixture on the lobster and the shrimp.

Blend all of the **vinaigrette** ingredients, except the oil, in a blender. While the motor is running, slowly add the oil and blend until smooth. To serve, dip the rim of 4 margarita glasses in water, then dip into chili powder. In the bottom of each glass, put about $\frac{1}{2}$ cup of salad greens, 3 shrimp, $\frac{1}{2}$ lobster tail, 1 claw, and 1 ounce crabmeat. Add $\frac{1}{4}$ cup fish dip to each glass. Drizzle the vinaigrette onto the seafood and stand a potato cracker in the fish dip. Garnish with chives and baby frisée. Serves 4.

CONCH FRITTERS

Dawn Sieber, Cheeca Lodge

Both the conch fritters and the Key lime mustard sauce are specialties of the Keys. Serve the fritters as appetizers or tidbits with cocktails.

Conch Fritters
 4 bacon strips, chopped
 1 red bell pepper, diced
 1 green pepper, diced
 1 large onion, diced
 1 teaspoon chopped garlic
 2 shallots, chopped
 4 celery ribs, sliced
 2 tablespoons chopped fresh basil
 $1/2$ bunch cilantro, chopped
 2 pounds cleaned conch, finely chopped
    or ground
 4 slices soft white bread, crumbed
 $1/4$ cup cornmeal
 2 tablespoons white flour
 1 tablespoon Old Bay Seasoning
 Pinch cayenne pepper
 1 teaspoon salt
 1 teaspoon black pepper
 2 eggs
 1 tablespoon half-and-half
 2 tablespoons chopped parsley
 Vegetable oil for frying

Key Lime Mustard Sauce
 1 cup mayonnaise
 $1/2$ cup Pommery mustard
 $1/2$ cup Dijon-style mustard
 Juice of 2 limes
 2 tablespoons Key lime oil

 2 tablespoons honey
 2 teaspoons chopped garlic
 Zest and juice of 1 orange

To make the **fritters**, sauté the bacon until crisp. Remove from the pan. Sauté the peppers, onion, garlic, shallots and celery in the drippings. Put the sauté mixture in a bowl to cool. Stir in the reserved bacon and the remaining ingredients, except the oil, and mix well. Form into 1- to $1^{1}/_{2}$-inch balls, and refrigerate to chill.

To make the **Key lime mustard sauce**, combine all the ingredients and mix well.

Just before serving, pan-fry the fritters in a couple of inches of oil over medium-high heat or deep-fry at 350°F until golden brown, about 5 minutes. Drain on paper towels. Serve with the mustard sauce or cocktail sauce. Yields 30 fritters.

BRAISED ARTICHOKES WITH SPINY LOBSTER

Jan Jorgensen, Soren Brendahl, Two Chefs Cooking

This is a light and elegant appetizer. The artichokes are filled with the meat of Florida spiny lobsters, then topped with a tomato hash and a hint of basil and truffle oil.

4 large artichokes
1 cup concentrated chicken stock
2 spiny lobster tails, approximately 1 1/4 pounds each (or substitute 1 1/2 pounds Maine lobster tails), blanched in boiling water
6 tablespoons unsalted butter
2 tomatoes, peeled, seeded, and diced
3 tablespoons chopped fresh basil
2 tablespoons white truffle oil
Salt and pepper to taste
Garnish: 1 leek, white part thinly sliced
Oil for deep frying

Boil the artichokes in salted water for 15 to 20 minutes or until the bottoms are tender when pierced with a wooden skewer. Remove them from the water, and when cool enough to handle, peel the outside leaves and fuzzy beards off, leaving only the bottom (heart). Cut the stem, leaving approximately 1/2 inch of stem base. Place in a pot with the chicken stock and set aside.

To prepare the lobster, cut the tail shell with poultry scissors to remove the tail meat. Cut the meat into medallions and sear with a little butter in a medium-hot skillet for 3 to 4 minutes, leaving the lobster meat medium cooked.

To assemble, heat the artichoke bottoms in the chicken stock over medium heat. Add 3 tablespoons of the butter and the tomatoes. Remove the artichokes and place on individual serving plates or bowls. Arrange the lobster meat inside each artichoke bottom. To finish the tomato hash, keep the tomato mixture over medium heat. Very slowly, add the remaining butter to the tomatoes, mixing rapidly as you do so. Add the basil and the truffle oil and season to taste with salt and pepper. Scoop the tomato hash over the artichokes and lobster medallions.

For the garnish, deep-fry the sliced leek in oil heated to 275°F for about 1 minute, or until browned. Remove and drain on absorbent paper. Top each dish with some of the leek. Serves 4.

LOBSTER QUESADILLAS

Allen Susser, Chef Allen's

This recipe jazzes up traditional quesadillas by adding Florida spiny lobster to the filling. Serve them for appetizers or snacks.

12 ounces cooked spiny lobster meat
(or other lobster), diced
1 red bell pepper, diced
1 yellow bell pepper, diced
1 small red onion, diced
1 cup cooked corn kernels
1 cup diced chayote
3 tablespoons chopped scallions
2 tablespoons chopped cilantro
1½ teaspoons ground cumin
1 teaspoon ground chili powder
½ teaspoon kosher salt
½ teaspoon crushed red pepper flakes
2 tablespoons sour cream
3¾ cups shredded white Cheddar cheese
2 tablespoons unsalted butter, room
temperature
12 (8-inch) flour tortillas

To prepare the filling, combine the lobster, bell peppers, onion, corn, and chayote in a nonreactive bowl and mix well. Add the scallions, cilantro, cumin, chili powder, salt, and red pepper flakes. Fold in the sour cream and ¾ cup of the cheese.

Preheat the oven to 450°F.

To make the quesadillas, butter one side of each tortilla. Turn them over and sprinkle with a little of the Cheddar cheese. Spread about ½ cup of the lobster mixture over the lower half of each tortilla. Sprinkle with the remaining cheese (a scant ¼ cup for each quesadilla). Fold the top half of the tortillas down over the filling, and place them on baking sheets lined with foil or parchment paper.

Bake for about 8 minutes or until golden brown. Remove the quesadillas from the oven and cut each in half. Serve immediately. Serves 12.

CRISPY FROG LEGS

Carmen Gonzalez

Marinade

2 garlic cloves, minced
$1\frac{1}{2}$ teaspoons salt
1 teaspoon extra-virgin olive oil
$\frac{1}{2}$ teaspoon white vinegar
12 medium or large frog legs, cleaned

Three Tomato Concasse

1 ripe tomato, peeled, seeded and diced
1 green tomato, peeled, seeded and diced
1 yellow tomato, peeled, seeded and diced
4 sprigs fresh thyme
1 tablespoon extra-virgin olive oil
$\frac{1}{2}$ teaspoon salt
Pinch of white pepper

Warm Coconut and Peanut Sauce

2 ($13\frac{1}{2}$-ounce) cans coconut milk
$\frac{1}{2}$ cup Taste of Thai peanut sauce powder

Frog Legs Fry

$1\frac{1}{2}$ cups all-purpose flour
$1\frac{1}{2}$ cups yellow cornmeal
1 tablespoon cayenne pepper
1 tablespoon Old Bay seasoning
2 quarts canola oil

Combine the garlic cloves, salt, olive oil, and vinegar and mix well. Rub the frog legs with the mixture and marinate in the refrigerator, covered, for 48 hours.

To prepare the **tomato concasse**, combine the tomatoes with the thyme, olive oil, salt, and pepper. Keep covered in the refrigerator until ready to serve.

When ready to cook the frog legs, prepare the **coconut and peanut sauce**. In a saucepan, heat the coconut milk. Whisk in the peanut sauce mix. Reduce the heat and simmer for 15 minutes. Keep warm.

Combine the flour, cornmeal, cayenne pepper, and Old Bay seasoning in a mixing bowl. In a deep saucepan or fryer, heat the canola oil to 375°F. Toss the frog legs with the cornmeal mixture. Carefully drop the frog legs one by one in the oil and deep-fry for about 4 minutes or until golden brown. Remove with a slotted spoon and place on paper towels to drain.

Serve the crispy frog legs with the tomato concasse and the warm coconut and peanut sauce on the side. Serves 4.

CARIBBEAN JERK CHICKEN SKEWERS

Cindy Hutson, Norma's On The Beach

Jerk seasoning is typically Jamaican fare. Many say that Arawak Indians used it long before the arrival of Columbus. There is an affinity for spicy seasoning in South Florida, and perhaps it's best to warn that, although jerk seasoning is absolutely delicious, it is full of hot peppers. Adjust the heat by varying the amount of jerk paste. The Papaya and Mango Salsa makes a cool contrast to the heat of the seasoning.

Roasted Garlic and Garlic Oil

5 large whole garlic bulbs
1½ teaspoons freshly ground black pepper
½ cup extra-virgin olive oil

Chicken Skewers

2 pounds boneless, skinless chicken breasts
Garlic oil (see above)

Marinade

2 sprigs fresh thyme, leaves stripped and stems discarded
4 to 6 scallions, chopped (the white and part of the green)
2 cloves Roasted Garlic, crushed (see above)
1 teaspoon grated lemon zest
¼ cup sesame oil
3 tablespoons soy sauce
1 to 2 tablespoons jerk paste
1 teaspoon freshly ground black pepper

Papaya and Mango Salsa

1 firm ripe papaya, peeled, seeded, and diced
1 mango, diced
3 scallions, finely chopped
½ teaspoon hot pepper sauce
1 tablespoon brown sugar
3 tablespoons fresh lime juice

Begin by making the **roasted garlic and garlic oil**. Preheat the oven to 350°F. Peel the garlic and cut off the tips. Place in a baking pan and sprinkle with pepper. Pour the oil over the garlic and bake for 30 minutes, or until the garlic is tender when pierced with a knife. Extra oil will keep refrigerated in a jar for about 2 weeks.

Slice each chicken breast into 4 to 6 strips, cutting on the bias. Weave the chicken onto 35 presoaked bamboo skewers and put them in a nonreactive shallow dish. Combine all the marinade ingredients and pour over the chicken, making sure that it is covered. Cover and marinate for at least 1 hour in the refrigerator.

Mix together all of the ingredients for the **papaya and mango salsa**. Cover and refrigerate. Preheat the grill or broiler. Brush the rack with the roasted garlic oil. Grill the chicken for 4 minutes on each side or until cooked through. Serve skewers with Papaya and Mango Salsa, and optionally with mesclun. Serves 6 to 8.

COLD VEGETABLE TERRINE IN CILANTRO ASPIC

Christophe Gerard, Twelve Twenty, The Tides Hotel

Tomato Coulis

1 pound very ripe tomatoes, quartered
2 tablespoons tomato paste
$1/4$ cup olive oil
1 teaspoon celery seeds
$1/4$ cup sherry vinegar
Salt and pepper

Cilantro Aspic

$1/2$ cup olive oil
2 cups carrot chunks
$1/2$ pound celery root, peeled and cut in chunks
2 cups celery chunks
1 cup coarsely chopped onions
2 cups coarsely chopped leeks
2 tablespoons rosemary
2 whole garlic bulbs, cut in half horizontally
1 quart white wine
2 tablespoons sea salt
2 bay leaves, crumbled
2 cups chopped fresh cilantro leaves
2 tablespoons ground coriander
3 tablespoons (3 packets) gelatin

Vegetables

1 large zucchini, cut in $1/4$-inch slices
Olive oil
6 to 8 carrots, peeled and halved
$1/2$ pound celery root, peeled and cut in $1/4$-inch slices
12 spears large, fresh, green asparagus, peeled
$1/4$ pound green beans, trimmed
Garnish: Lemon thyme

Blend all of the **tomato coulis** ingredients in a blender, then strain, cool, and set aside.

For the **aspic**, heat the oil in an 8-quart stockpot over medium heat. Add the vegetables, rosemary, and garlic. Cook for about 2 minutes, stirring frequently. Add cold water to cover. Bring to a boil and simmer for 20 to 30 minutes, covered. Add the wine and the salt, cover, and continue to simmer for 20 to 30 minutes more. Remove from the heat and let sit for 15 minutes. When cool enough to handle, strain into a saucepan and boil to reduce to about 3 pints. Add the cilantro and coriander. Cool, strain, add the gelatin, and set aside.

Brush the zucchini with oil and grill for 3 minutes, or until soft, then cool. Boil the carrots in a saucepan for 10 minutes, or until soft. Drain, chill in ice water, and drain. Repeat for the other vegetables: boil the celery root for 15 minutes, the asparagus for 3 minutes, and the green beans for 5 minutes.

Line a 1-quart terrine with plastic wrap. Layer the vegetables, with the carrots on the bottom. Add 3 tablespoons of the aspic, then the celery root, 3 tablespoons of aspic, and so on until the vegetables are used. Pour aspic over all the vegetables to fill the terrine. Refrigerate for 24 hours to set. To serve, use the plastic wrap to lift the terrine out of the mold. Spoon some tomato coulis on a plate, add a slice of terrine and drizzle olive oil around the side. Garnish with a little lemon thyme. Serves 6.

JAMAICAN SEAFOOD SOUP

Dawn Sieber, Cheeca Lodge

This spicy soup makes good use of the fresh seafood that is so abundant in the Keys. The seafood is cooked separately, then added to the soup to prevent overcooking. Use whatever crabmeat is available if you can't get stone crabs. Jerk seasoning is very spicy, so begin with a small amount and increase it according to your taste.

> **2 ounces (about 2 slices) apple-smoked bacon or other smoked bacon, chopped**
> **$^1/_4$ cup diced onion**
> **$^1/_4$ cup diced celery**
> **$^1/_4$ cup diced leeks**
> **2 tablespoons dark brown sugar**
> **Pinch cayenne pepper**
> **1 teaspoon Jamaican jerk seasoning or to taste**
> **2 cups fish stock**
> **2 cups diced fresh plum tomatoes (about 1 pound)**
> **$^1/_2$ bunch tarragon ($^1/_2$ ounce), leaves removed and chopped**
> **Salt**
> **6 tablespoons unsalted butter**
> **$^1/_4$ pound medium shrimp, peeled, deveined, and chopped**
> **$^1/_4$ pound stone crabmeat, picked over and chopped**
> **$^1/_4$ pound snapper, dolphinfish (mahimahi), or grouper fillet, chopped**
> **Garnish: croutons, sliced scallions, or yogurt**

In a sauté pan, cook the bacon until crisp. Remove from the pan and drain. To the drippings in the pan, add the onion, celery, and leeks. Cook over low heat for 15 minutes until translucent. Stir in the brown sugar and continue to cook for 3 minutes. Add the cayenne and jerk seasoning and cook for 1 minute. Pour in the fish stock and the tomatoes. Simmer for 30 minutes. Add the tarragon and salt to taste.

Heat the butter in a small pan over low heat and add the seafood. Cook for a few minutes until done. To serve, put some of the seafood in each soup bowl along with your choice of a garnish, and top with the hot soup. Serves 4.

CARIBBEAN PUMPKIN BISQUE & CROSTINI

Cindy Hutson, Norma's On The Beach

CARIBBEAN PUMPKIN BISQUE

Calabaza is similar to the North American pumpkin, with a delicate flavor like a butternut or Hubbard squash, all of which are good substitutes. Calabaza is usually sold in wedges and is fabulous in stews or soups like this simple one.

- 1 tablespoon unsalted butter, or herbed butter
- 1 large onion, sliced
- 2 sprigs fresh thyme, leaves stripped off stems and stems discarded
- $1/4$ large calabaza, peeled, seeded, and diced (4 cups)
- 1 garlic clove, crushed
- 1 carrot, sliced
- 1 smoked ham hock
- 2 quarts chicken stock
- $1/2$ Scotch bonnet pepper, seeded (or more to taste)
- Salt and freshly ground black pepper

Heat the butter in a large stock pot. Add the onion and sauté until translucent and wilted, but not brown, about 4 minutes. Add the thyme leaves to the pot along with the calabaza, garlic, and carrot. Sauté until tender, about 4 minutes. Add the ham hock and pour in the chicken stock. Bring to a boil, and cook for 10 minutes. Drop in the hot pepper. Reduce the heat and simmer, covered, for 45 minutes. Uncover and remove the ham hock and the hot pepper. Let cool for 15 minutes.

In a blender or food processor, blend in small batches until smooth and creamy. Add salt and pepper to taste. Serve hot. Makes 3 quarts.

CROSTINI

Garlic fans will enjoy these on their own or as an accompaniment to soups and salads.

- 1 loaf crusty French, Italian, or Cuban bread, cut in $1/4$-inch slices

Garlic Paste
- 3 whole garlic bulbs, peeled and ends cut off
- 1 cup canola oil

Herb Butter
- $1/2$ pound salted butter, at room temperature
- 2 tablespoons finely chopped fresh chives
- 3 scallions, finely chopped
- $1/4$ cup finely chopped parsley

To make the **garlic paste**, combine the garlic and oil in a blender and puree into a smooth paste. Store in an airtight container in the refrigerator and use as needed.

To make the **herb butter**, combine the butter with the chives, scallions, and 2 tablespoons garlic paste. Add the parsley and beat at low speed until mixed.

Spread the slices of bread with the herb butter. Place them on a sheet pan and broil until golden brown. Serve at once. Serves 6 to 8.

KEYS CONCH CHOWDER

Fresh milk was scarce and refrigeration a challenge in the Florida Keys in the nineteenth century, so when canned evaporated milk was introduced in about 1885, it was adopted for use in conch chowder and other dishes. Those are no longer issues, of course, but this version uses coconut milk, another canned product, to add a tropical sweetness and a chili pepper for a flavor boost. The recipe multiplies easily for a crowd.

$1/4$ **pound salt pork, sliced**
1 onion, finely chopped
$1/2$ **cup finely chopped celery**
1 carrot, finely chopped
1 tomato, peeled, seeded, and chopped
1 potato, peeled and diced
1 garlic clove, minced
1 pound conch, pounded and cut into
  $1/2$**-inch cubes**
1 (13$1/2$-ounce) can coconut milk
2 cups water
1$1/2$ teaspoons salt
$1/4$ **teaspoon freshly ground black pepper**
1 teaspoon dried thyme
2 bay leaves
1 Scotch bonnet pepper

In a large saucepan, fry the salt pork slowly to render the fat. Remove the pork from the pan and discard. In the remaining fat, sauté the onion, celery, and carrot for 5 minutes, then add the tomato, potato, garlic, and conch. Cook for an additional 3 minutes. Add the remaining ingredients and stir thoroughly. Cover and reduce the heat to low. Simmer for 1$1/2$ hours, or until the conch is tender. Add additional water if the chowder becomes too thick. Remove and discard the bay leaves and Scotch bonnet pepper. Serve hot. Serves 4 to 6.

CHILLED CHAYOTE SOUP

Doug Shook, Louie's Backyard

Historians tell us that the chayote (a.k.a. mirliton or christophene) has been eaten for centuries and was one of the staples of the Aztecs and Mayans of Mexico and South America. It is commonplace in South Florida markets and is delightful and refreshing in this soup. The soft seed is edible and can be cooked along with the rest of the squash.

    4 chayote squash, peeled and cut into chunks
    1 large onion, cut into chunks
    1 Granny Smith apple, peeled and quartered
    1 bay leaf
    1 sprig thyme
    1 sprig mint
    1 quart chicken stock, chicken broth or water
    1 cup plain low-fat yogurt
    Salt and pepper

Garnish
    $^1/_2$ cup very thinly sliced red radishes
    $^1/_2$ cup thinly sliced young, slender carrots
    $^1/_2$ cup thinly sliced young green beans,
        blanched
    $^1/_2$ cup thinly sliced sugar snap peas, blanched
    $^1/_2$ cup snipped chives ($^1/_2$-inch lengths)
    $^1/_2$ cup fresh mint leaves
    $^1/_2$ cup ($^1/_4$-inch square) croutons (firm white
        bread cubes, toasted)
    6 tablespoons plain low-fat yogurt

To make the soup, combine the squash, onion, apple, herbs, and stock in a saucepan. Bring to a simmer and cook until the vegetables are very tender, about 15 minutes. Working in batches, puree in a blender or food processor. Strain into a bowl. Cover and refrigerate until cool. Stir in 1 cup yogurt, and salt and pepper to taste. Refrigerate until chilled.

To serve, ladle the soup into wide bowls. Scatter the remaining vegetables, herbs, and croutons over the soup and top each serving with a spoonful of yogurt. Serves 6.

SPANISH BEAN SOUP

This is a very popular Spanish bean soup made with garbanzo beans, chorizo sausage, potatoes, and a hint of saffron. If you like, cook the beans with a ham hock, then cut up and add the bits of meat to the soup at the end. In a pinch, some people use strips of bacon in place of the salt pork.

1 pound dried garbanzo beans (chickpeas)
2 (14$\frac{1}{2}$-ounce) cans beef stock or broth
2 (14$\frac{1}{2}$-ounce) cans chicken stock or broth
2 quarts water
4 bay leaves
$\frac{1}{4}$ pound salt pork, cut into $\frac{1}{4}$-inch strips
2 garlic cloves, minced
2 onions, diced
$\frac{1}{2}$ red bell pepper, diced
3 medium-size potatoes, peeled and cubed
$\frac{1}{2}$ teaspoon black pepper
$\frac{1}{2}$ teaspoon paprika
$\frac{1}{2}$ teaspoon saffron
2 (3-ounce) chorizo sausages, thinly sliced
Salt

Pick through the dried beans and remove any foreign pieces. Place the beans in a large saucepan with 2 quarts of water, and soak overnight (or quick soak according to package directions). Drain the beans and discard the water.

Place the beans in a 6-quart stock pot. Add the beef stock, chicken stock, 1 quart of the water, and the bay leaves. Cover and cook over medium-high heat. While the beans are cooking, fry the salt pork to render the fat, approximately 10 minutes. Add the garlic, onions, and pepper and cook 5 minutes longer. Remove from the heat and set aside.

After the beans have cooked for 1 hour, add the additional 1 quart of water, the vegetable mixture, and the remaining ingredients to the pot. Cook until the potatoes are soft, about 30 minutes. Skim the fat from the top of the soup and remove the salt pork and bay leaves before serving. Season with salt to taste. Serves 8 to 10.

BLACK BEAN SOUP

Black beans are ubiquitous on Cuban restaurant menus in Miami, served both as soup and as a side dish with white rice. The beans, also known as turtle beans, are actually a dark purple color. This soup can be a meal in itself, and is especially good topped with a dollop of sour cream and a sprinkling of chopped onions. If there is any soup left over, its robust flavor will be even better the next day.

1 pound dried black beans
1 smoked ham hock
3 quarts water
2 onions, diced
1 red bell pepper, diced
1 green bell pepper, diced
2 tablespoons olive oil
4 garlic cloves, minced
2 bay leaves
1$\frac{1}{2}$ teaspoons dried oregano
1 teaspoon ground cumin
1 tablespoon salt
$\frac{1}{2}$ teaspoon black pepper
2 tablespoons chopped fresh cilantro
$\frac{1}{4}$ teaspoon ground cloves
2 teaspoons sugar
4 tablespoons dry sherry or 1 tablespoon
   wine vinegar
Sour cream
Finely chopped scallions
Finely chopped cilantro

Pick through the dried beans and remove any foreign pieces. Soak the beans overnight in 2 quarts of water (or quick-soak according to the package directions). Discard the water and rinse the beans.

Place the beans in a 6-quart stockpot with the ham hock and 3 quarts of water. Bring to a boil over high heat. Cover the pot and reduce the heat to medium-high.

While the beans are cooking, sauté the onions and bell peppers in olive oil in a nonstick skillet over medium heat and until softened but not browned, about 15 minutes. Add the garlic, bay leaves, oregano, cumin, salt, pepper, cilantro, and cloves. Sauté for 2 minutes longer. Set aside off the heat. When the beans have cooked for 1 hour, remove the ham hock. Stir the sautéed vegetables and sugar into the beans. Reduce the heat and simmer, covered, for 45 minutes. Remove the meat from the ham hock, chop, and add to the beans. Add the dry sherry or wine vinegar to the beans and simmer for 15 minutes longer. Remove the bay leaves.

To serve, garnish each bowl of soup with sour cream, chopped onion, and cilantro. Serves 6 to 8.

CUBAN SANDWICH & GREEN PLANTAIN SOUP

CUBAN SANDWICH

This is one of Cuban Miami's most popular sandwiches, and it is absolutely delicious. You'll often see them ready-made and piled high in restaurants and takeout shops, waiting to be warmed in a sandwich press. The filling can vary tremendously, but they all have baked ham, roasted pork, Swiss cheese, and dill pickles. You can spread mustard, oil, butter, or even garlicky mojo on the sandwich bread.

> 1 loaf Cuban bread, 8 to 9 inches long
> Yellow mustard, olive oil, softened butter or Mojo Marinade (page 31)
> $1/4$ pound sliced baked ham
> $1/4$ pound sliced lean roasted pork
> 2 ounces sliced Swiss cheese
> Sliced dill pickles

Slice the bread lengthwise and brush with mustard or another spread. Arrange the ham, pork, cheese, and pickle slices in layers on one side of the bread. Cover with the other piece of bread.

Toast in a sandwich press, waffle iron, or sauté pan to warm the bread and slightly melt the cheese. Cut diagonally into wedges. Serves 2.

GREEN PLANTAIN SOUP

Though they are a type of banana, plantains must be cooked before they are eaten. For this superb soup, fried plantain slices are added to a garlic-laced chicken stock and cooked until the plantains fall apart and thicken the soup. Watch the soup carefully to prevent it from sticking to the pot.

> 6 cups rich chicken stock
> 2 garlic cloves, minced
> $1/4$ cup vegetable oil
> 3 green plantains, peeled and cut in $1/2$-inch diagonal slices
> Salt and pepper

In a saucepan, bring the chicken stock to a boil. Add the garlic and simmer. Meanwhile, heat the oil in a large skillet over medium heat. Working in batches if necessary, fry the plantains until they are tender and brown on both sides, 8 to 10 minutes. As they are cooked, drain them on paper towels and add them to the boiling stock. Reduce the heat and simmer, partially covered, for 15 to 20 minutes, stirring often to break up and mash the plantains and to prevent sticking. Season to taste with salt and pepper, and add more stock if you prefer a thinner consistency. Serve hot. Serves 6 to 8.

Helpful hint: To peel a green plantain, take a small knife and slit through the skin from tip to tip of the plantain in several places. Then peel each strip from the fruit.

CAESAR SALAD WITH CRISPY OYSTERS

Carmen Gonzalez

The dressing stores well in the refrigerator for a few days if you don't use it all, and it can be made ahead of time. Fry the oysters at the last minute so they will be hot and crisp.

Croutons and Salad

    Vegetable oil
    1 loaf French bread, cut into $^1/_2$-inch cubes
    1 head Romaine lettuce, torn into bite-size
        pieces

Caesar Dressing

    2 garlic cloves, peeled
    10 anchovies (about one 2-ounce tin, drained)
    Juice of 1 lemon
    $^1/_3$ cup grated Parmigiano-Reggiano cheese
    $^3/_4$ cup salad oil
    6 tablespoons olive oil
    2 eggs
    $^1/_4$ teaspoon salt
    $^1/_4$ teaspoon freshly ground black pepper

Spicy Crispy Oysters

    $^3/_4$ cup white flour
    $^3/_4$ cup cornmeal
    $1^1/_2$ teaspoons cayenne pepper
    $1^1/_2$ teaspoons Old Bay seasoning
    Vegetable oil for frying
    24 oysters, scrubbed and shucked

To make the **croutons**, heat the oil in a sauté pan over medium heat. Add the bread cubes and brown, tossing occasionally to prevent scorching. Drain on paper towels and set aside.

To prepare the **dressing**, combine the garlic, anchovies, lemon juice, and cheese in a food processor or blender and process to make a paste. Add the oils in a slow stream. Then add the eggs, salt, and pepper. Process until smooth. Refrigerate until chilled.

To make the **crispy oysters**, mix together the flour, cornmeal, cayenne and Old Bay seasoning. Heat about 2 inches of oil in a deep pan to 375°F. Toss the oysters in the cornmeal mixture, then add to the hot oil and cook until golden brown. Remove from the oil and drain on paper towels.

To assemble the salad, toss the lettuce with enough dressing to moisten, and divide it among 4 salad plates. Top each salad with hot oysters and sprinkle with croutons and cheese shavings, if desired. Serve immediately, with additional dressing on the side. Serves 4.

ACHIOTE-MARINATED GRILLED CHICKEN SALAD

Paul Gjertson, Deering Bay Yacht & Country Club

You'll find lots of citrus in Miami recipes. Here, the orange and grapefruit sections complement the grilled chicken nicely, as do the rich, zesty flavors of the marinade and the dressing.

1 cup vegetable oil
3 tablespoons fresh lemon juice
1 tablespoon achiote paste
2 teaspoons chopped garlic
3 tablespoons grated Spanish onion
4 (5-ounce) boneless chicken breasts
Salt and freshly ground black pepper
2 bunches arugula, trimmed and chilled
   (about 4 cups)

Dressing
$1/2$ teaspoon lime zest
2 tablespoons fresh lime juice
1 teaspoon chopped garlic
$1/4$ habanero pepper, seeded
2 tablespoons chopped cilantro
$3/4$ cup vegetable oil
3 tablespoons feta cheese

Garnish
12 orange segments
12 grapefruit segments
1 mango, peeled and cut into 8 equal slices

In a large nonreactive mixing bowl, whisk the oil, lemon juice, achiote paste, garlic, and onion until fully blended. Add the chicken breasts, cover and refrigerate overnight. Prepare the **dressing** by processing all the ingredients in a blender until thoroughly mixed. Refrigerate until chilled.

Heat a grill or broiler until very hot. Remove the chicken from the marinade and season with salt and pepper. Grill or broil until cooked through and golden brown, about 4 to 5 minutes per side.

To serve, place about 1 cup of arugula greens on the side of 4 serving plates. For each serving, arrange 1 breast of chicken and garnish with 3 orange segments, 3 grapefruit segments, and 2 slices of mango. Spoon 2 tablespoons of the dressing over each salad and serve the remaining dressing on the side. Serves 4.

CARIBBEAN SPINY LOBSTER SALAD

Pascal Oudin, Sweet Donna's Country Store Restaurant & Bakery

This is an elegant and satisfying salad that combines Florida spiny lobsters and portobello mushrooms in a Key lime and coconut vinaigrette. Accompany this dish with Fried Yuca Cubes (recipe, page 137).

1 bunch red oak lettuce
1 bunch green oak lettuce
8 chive stems, plus 4 chive stems, blanched
2 whole spiny lobsters (1$\frac{1}{2}$ pounds each) or 2 Maine lobsters (1 pound each)
4 medium-size portobello mushrooms, stems removed
$\frac{1}{4}$ cup olive oil
2 garlic cloves, chopped
Salt and freshly ground black pepper

Key Lime Coconut Vinaigrette
1 cup orange juice
$\frac{1}{4}$ cup Key lime juice
$\frac{1}{4}$ cup coconut milk
1 cup olive oil
$\frac{1}{2}$ tablespoon finely chopped shallots
$\frac{1}{4}$ teaspoon freshly ground black pepper
Sea salt
Crushed red peppercorns

Divide the salad greens and chives into 4 portions and use the blanched chives to tie the mounds into bundles. Set aside in the refrigerator.

Bring a large, deep pot of water to a boil and plunge the lobsters in head first. Cover and cook for 5 minutes. Remove the lobsters and cool under cold water, or set aside to cool in a colander. Crack the shells, remove the meat, then cover and refrigerate.

Toss the mushroom caps with the olive oil and garlic, mixing well. Add salt and pepper to taste. Place in a roasting pan and cover with foil. Bake in a preheated 400°F oven for 15 minutes, or until thoroughly cooked. Set aside to cool for 5 minutes. With a 1-inch round cutter, cut out the center of each mushroom, giving it a donut shape.

For the **vinaigrette**, in a small saucepan over medium heat, reduce the orange juice by one-third, to $\frac{2}{3}$ cup. Add 3 tablespoons of the lime juice and 2 tablespoons of the coconut milk. Slowly whisk in the olive oil, the remaining coconut milk, and more lime juice to taste. Stir in the chopped shallots, the black pepper, salt, and crushed red peppercorn to taste. Keep at a warm temperature until ready to serve.

To assemble the salad, set the mushrooms in the center of the plate. Place the bundles of greens upright in the hole of the mushroom. Cut each lobster tail in half lengthwise and place in the center of a mushroom. Drizzle the warm vinaigrette all the way down the plate and over the lobster. Arrange the fried yuca cubes around the edge of the salads. Serves 4.

Caribbean Spiny Lobster Salad with Fried Yuca Cubes

JEREZ SHERRY SPIKED LOBSTER GAZPACHO

Todd Weisz, Turnberry Isle Resort & Club

Spanish gazpacho is a classic cold pureed tomato and vegetable soup, with bell peppers, cucumbers, and tomatoes being the primary ingredients. This light, contemporary version is actually more of a gazpacho-style salad, featuring the same vegetables to complement the lobster, plantains, and salad greens. Maine lobsters often are used in South Florida since local spiny lobsters can be hard to find. The Florida lobsters are only in season for six months, but Maine lobsters are available in most grocery stores.

2 (1½-pound) Maine lobsters

Gazpacho
    1 large red bell pepper, chopped (about 1 cup)
    1 fresh tomato, peeled, seeded, and chopped
        (about 1½ cups)
    ½ cup peeled, seeded and chopped cucumber
    1 tablespoon sherry wine vinegar
    1 teaspoon salt
    ¼ teaspoon freshly ground black pepper
    2 tablespoons extra-virgin olive oil

Oil for deep-frying
1 green plantain
Salt
2 cups assorted salad greens and green beans
8 to 10 chive sprigs
½ cup currant tomatoes, halved, or cherry
    tomatoes, quartered
Garnish: Sunflower sprouts

Plunge the lobsters, head first, into a large pot of boiling water and cook for 7 to 10 minutes. Remove from the pot and place in a large bowl of ice water to cool. When the lobster is cool, crack the shell and carefully remove the meat. Cut each lobster tail into 4 slices. Cover the lobster meat and refrigerate.

To make the gazpacho, combine all of the ingredients in a blender. Blend until smooth, strain through a fine strainer, cover, and chill.

Just before serving, heat oil in a deep-fryer or tall, heavy saucepan to 350°F. Peel the plantain and slice thinly lengthwise; they will be slightly sticky. Roll each strip into a 2-inch ring and pinch the ends so they stick together. The natural starch of the green plantain will hold the ring together. Deep-fry until golden brown, about 3 to 4 minutes. Place on absorbent paper and sprinkle with salt.

To serve, arrange the green beans, salad greens, and a couple of chives inside each plantain ring in 4 chilled soup plates. Place the lobster tail along the edge of the bowl and a lobster claw in the middle. Arrange the beans and tomatoes around the plate and spoon the gazpacho on to the plate, approximately ½ cup per serving. Garnish with fresh basil and sunflower sprouts. Serves 4.

CRISPY CHILEAN SEA BASS

Todd Weisz, Turnberry Isle Resort & Club

Parmesan Tuile

6 tablespoons high-quality grated Parmesan cheese (such as Parmigiano-Reggiano)

Nicoise Potatoes

2 large potatoes, peeled and cut into chunks
$\frac{1}{2}$ to $\frac{3}{4}$ cup whipping cream
2 tablespoons unsalted butter
2 tablespoons pitted and pureed Nicoise olives
1 teaspoon salt
$\frac{1}{4}$ teaspoon freshly ground black pepper

Tomato Coulis

$1\frac{1}{2}$ cups tomatoes, peeled, seeded, and chopped
$\frac{1}{2}$ cup chopped onion
1 tablespoon minced garlic
1 cup chicken broth
1 teaspoon salt
$\frac{1}{4}$ teaspoon freshly ground black pepper
1 tablespoon unsalted butter
3 fresh basil leaves

4 (6-ounce) sea bass fillets, with skin on
Salt and freshly ground black pepper
2 to 3 tablespoons olive oil
1 cup baby arugula
4 chives

For the **tuile**, preheat the oven to 350°F. On a non-stick baking pan, sprinkle cheese in four thin, 6-inch long oval layers. Spray the cheese generously with a fine mist of water and bake for 5 minutes. It will bubble and turn slightly golden. Remove and cool.

Put the **potatoes** in a medium pot with water to cover. Bring to a boil over high heat, then reduce to a simmer. Cook for 10 to 15 minutes, or until tender. Drain and let stand for 5 minutes. Press the potatoes through a ricer or food mill. In a saucepan, bring the cream and butter to a simmer. Add to the potatoes, then add the olive puree, salt, and pepper. Stir slowly until the mixture is smooth.

To make the **tomato coulis**, combine all the ingredients except the butter and basil in a saucepan; simmer for 30 minutes. Remove from the heat. Put the mixture in a blender, add the butter and basil, and blend until smooth. Keep warm.

Preheat the oven to 350°F. Season the sea bass on both sides with salt and pepper. Heat the olive oil in an ovenproof sauté pan over high heat. Add the fillets, skin side down. When the skin starts to brown and become crisp, place the pan in the oven and bake for 5 to 10 minutes, depending on the thickness of the fillet. The meat should be white and firm. Remove the pan from the oven.

For each plate, spoon $\frac{1}{2}$ cup potatoes into a 3-inch ring and press down to form a small cake. Unmold on each serving plate. Place the fish, skin side up, on top. Arrange the baby arugula around the fish and spoon the coulis on the plate. Stand a Parmesan Tuile in the potatoes and garnish with a single chive. Serves 4.

SEA BASS WITH LOBSTER AND PLANTAINS

Efrain Veiga, Yuca

2 (1½-pound) lobsters
2 cups young lettuce

Lobster-Mirin Broth

2 tablespoons olive oil
1 small onion, chopped
1 cup chopped celery
2 small tomatoes, chopped
2 cups mirin (a type of sweet rice wine)
Salt and pepper
6 cilantro sprigs

Avocado Salsa

1 avocado, diced
2 large tomatoes, diced
1 onion, diced
1 tablespoon chopped cilantro
1 teaspoon lemon juice
1 teaspoon minced jalapeño
Salt and pepper

Glazed Plantains

2 ripe plantains, peeled
¼ cup honey
1 teaspoon cinnamon

Sea Bass

Salt and pepper
4 (4-ounce) sea bass fillets
¼ cup black sesame seeds
3 teaspoons vegetable oil

Blanch the lobsters in boiling water for 1 minute. Crack the shells and remove and set aside the meat.

In a large saucepan, combine lobster shells, olive oil, onions, and celery over medium-high heat and sauté briefly. Cover with water, add the tomatoes and mirin, and bring to a boil. Reduce the heat and simmer for 1 hour. Season with salt and pepper to taste and add the cilantro sprigs. Keep warm.

In salted, boiling water, cook the meat from the lobster tails for 3 minutes and the rest of the meat for 6 minutes. Remove and set aside.

Combine all of the **salsa** ingredients in a bowl and mix well. Season with salt and pepper.

Preheat the oven to 350°F. Combine the **plantains** with the cinnamon and honey in a shallow baking dish. Bake for 12 minutes. Remove from the oven and cut in half lengthwise. Set aside.

Season both sides of each **sea bass** fillet with salt and pepper. Sprinkle one side of each fillet with sesame seeds and gently pat them on. Heat a sauté pan with the vegetable oil over high heat. Add the fillets, one at a time, with the sesame crust down, and sauté for 2 minutes. Turn the fish and sauté for 2 minutes on the other side.

To serve, strain the broth. Place a plantain half on each plate and arrange some of the lettuce alongside. Place the fish on the lettuce and spoon about ½ cup of the the avocado salsa next to the fish. Cut the lobster meat into chunks and scatter them around the plate. Ladle ¼ cup of hot broth onto each plate and serve at once. Serves 4.

BARBECUED SALMON

Johnny Vinczencz, Astor Place, Johnny V's Kitchen

Barbecue Spice Mix

6 tablespoons paprika
3 tablespoons ancho chile powder
1 tablespoon ground cumin
1 tablespoon ground coriander
1 tablespoon sugar
1 tablespoon black pepper
1 tablespoon California Molido or other red
  chile powder
1 tablespoon salt

Barbecue Glaze

$1/4$ cup sugar
$1/4$ cup water
3 tablespoons Barbecue Spice Mix (see above)

Papaya Applesauce

5 Granny Smith apples, peeled and cored
1 papaya, peeled and seeded
2 cups apple juice
$1/4$ teaspoon cinnamon
$1/8$ teaspoon nutmeg
2 tablespoons brown sugar

Corn and Pea Salad

3 ears of corn, cooked and cut off the cob
$1^1/_2$ cups green peas, cooked and plunged in
  cold water
3 tablespoons diced red onion
3 tablespoons dried red pepper, cut in $1/_4$ inch
  dice
2 tablespoons vegetable oil
Salt and pepper to taste

4 (7-ounce) salmon fillets
$1/_2$ cup Barbecue Spice Mix (see above)
$1/_2$ cup vegetable oil
Potato Latkes (page 136)
Garnish: Sour cream and chives

To make the **barbecue spice mix**, combine all of the ingredients in a small mixing bowl. To make the **barbecue glaze**, mix the sugar, water and 3 tablespoons of the barbecue spice in a saucepan and bring to a boil. Lower the heat and simmer for about 15 minutes or until it has become syrupy. Set aside.

To make the **papaya applesauce**, combine all of the ingredients in a saucepan and cook over medium heat until the fruit is soft. Drain the liquid and discard. Mash the fruit with a potato masher until the mixture is not quite smooth. Set aside.

To make the **corn and pea salad**, mix all the ingredients in a mixing bowl, cover and chill.

In a hot cast iron skillet, sear the salmon on both sides for about 2 minutes. Transfer to a preheated 375°F oven and bake for 3 to 4 minutes. Remove from the oven and brush with barbecue glaze. Return to the oven and bake for another 3 to 4 minutes, or until medium rare. Do not turn the salmon.

To serve, arrange the salmon, potato latkes, papaya applesauce, and corn and pea salad on individual dinner plates. Garnish the potato latkes with a dollop of sour cream and a sprig of chives. Serves 4.

SWORDFISH WITH MANGO SCOTCH BONNET SAUCE

Mark Militello, Mark's Las Olas

Mango Scotch Bonnet Sauce
  2 green bell peppers, halved and seeded
  2 red bell peppers, halved and seeded
  4 fresh peeled tomatoes, halved and seeded
  3 ripe mangos, peeled and chopped
  1 onion, chopped
  2 tablespoons chopped garlic (4 to 5 cloves), minced
  2 scotch bonnet peppers, cut in half
  $^3/_4$ cup cider vinegar
  1 cup brown sugar
  $^1/_4$ cup molasses
  $^1/_4$ cup Dijon mustard
  $^1/_4$ cup tamarind pulp
  2 tablespoons cinnamon
  1 tablespoon cumin
  1 tablespoon thyme leaf
  1 tablespoon marjoram
  Salt and freshly ground black pepper
  1 cup water

  4 (8-ounce) swordfish steaks
  Olive oil
  Salt and freshly ground black pepper
  2 chayotes, cut into $^1/_4$-inch slices

Avocado Butter
  2 ripe avocados
  Juice of $^1/_2$ lime
  $^1/_4$ cup extra-virgin olive oil
  Salt and freshly ground black pepper

To make the **sauce**, combine all of the ingredients in a large nonreactive saucepan. Simmer gently for 1 hour. Remove from the heat and let cool slightly. Puree the sauce in a blender or food processor and pour it through a medium mesh strainer. Correct the seasoning, adding salt and pepper to taste.

Brush the swordfish with olive oil and sprinkle with salt and pepper. Set aside.

To prepare the **avocado butter**, cut the avocados in half and scrape out the flesh. Puree the flesh in a food processor or blender with the lime juice, slowly adding the olive oil, salt and pepper. Set aside.

Prepare a medium fire in a grill. Brush the chayote with olive oil and grill over medium heat for several minutes until tender. Remove and set aside. Grill the swordfish, continually basting with the sauce.

To serve, arrange the chayote slices in circles on dinner plates. Place the swordfish in the center. Garnish each piece of fish with a tablespoon of avocado butter and serve at once. Serves 4.

GRILLED WAHOO WITH CURRIED CONCH STEW

Jan Jorgensen, Soren Bredahl, Two Chefs Cooking

A member of the mackerel family, wahoo (with its amusing name) is considered by many to be the fastest fish in the sea. Swordfish or sea bass may be substituted in this recipe. Thinly sliced conch and vegetables are combined in a coconut milk curry stew that is served alongside the grilled fish. Conch is very tough, so make sure to slice the meat in very thin slices.

> **4 (8-ounce) wahoo fillets**
> **Olive oil**
> **Fresh basil stems**
> **1 stalk lemongrass, roughly chopped**
> **Salt and pepper**

Curried Conch Stew

> **Oil**
> **1 pound conch meat, very thinly sliced**
> **1 carrot, finely diced**
> **1 onion, finely diced**
> **1 celery rib, finely diced**
> **Kernels cut from 1 ear of corn**
> **2 tablespoons Indian curry paste**
> **1 cup chicken stock**
> **1 ($14\frac{1}{2}$-ounce) can coconut milk (about 2 cups)**
> **2 tomatoes, peeled, seeded and chopped**
> **2 tablespoons chopped fresh rosemary**
> **2 tablespoons chopped fresh thyme**
> **Garnish: $\frac{1}{4}$ cup finely chopped parsley**

In a shallow dish big enough to hold the fish in one layer, add enough olive oil to coat the bottom. Add the basil and lemongrass and marinate the fillets in the refrigerator for 5 to 6 hours, turning occasionally.

To prepare the **conch stew**, heat a little oil in a large sauté pan over medium-high heat. Add the conch meat and sauté for about 30 seconds, or until tender. Remove and reserve. In the same pan, sauté the carrot, onion, celery, and corn for 5 to 6 minutes. Add the curry paste and cook for another minute. Deglaze with the chicken stock and cook for 5 minutes. Add the coconut milk, tomatoes, and fresh herbs. Cook the stew for another 5 minutes. Add the sautéed conch, bring to a boil for 2 to 3 minutes. Reduce to low while you cook the fish.

To cook the fish, prepare a medium fire in a grill. Wipe the marinade from the fish, season with salt and pepper, and grill for 4 to 5 minutes on each side, brushing often with the marinade.

To serve, spoon the curried conch stew in large soup bowls and place a wahoo fillet on top of each bowl of stew. Garnish with the parsley. Serves 4.

STEAMED HALIBUT

Jonathan Eismann, Pacific Time

This makes a light and attractive main course. Individual sealed baking dishes allow guests to enjoy the aromas as they open their own pans. Use ovenproof dishes that are 8 to 10 inches in diameter and at least $1\frac{1}{2}$ inches high. You can also use a larger pan, even a foil one, and transfer the cooked fish to individual serving bowls. Halibut may be replaced with any white flaky fish such as turbot, large sole, or flounder.

- 3 tablespoons extra-virgin olive oil
- 6 teaspoons finely minced fresh ginger
- $4\frac{1}{2}$ cups peeled, seeded and chopped tomatoes, undrained
- 1 cup fresh cilantro leaves, no stems
- Finely ground sea salt and freshly ground white pepper
- 6 skinless, center-cut halibut fillets, 1 to $1\frac{1}{2}$ inches thick
- 9 tablespoons fresh lemon juice
- 3 tablespoons fresh lime juice
- 12 fresh lemongrass bulbs, julienned (bulbs only)
- 12 fresh lime leaves (optional)
- 3 large leeks, whites only, julienned
- $1\frac{1}{2}$ tablespoons minced Italian parsley
- $1\frac{1}{2}$ teaspoons finely grated lemon zest
- 1 cup Japanese cold seaweed salad (hiyashe wakame) available prepared in Japanese grocery stores

Rub the bottoms of 6 ovenproof baking dishes with the olive oil and sprinkle with the ginger. Mound $\frac{3}{4}$ cup tomatoes in the center of each dish. Arrange about $2\frac{1}{2}$ tablespoons of cilantro leaves on top of each mound, and lightly season with salt and pepper. Season the halibut fillets on both sides with salt, and on the skin side with pepper. Place the fillets on top of the tomatoes, skin side down. Mix the citrus juices together and pour 2 tablespoons over each fillet. Divide the lemongrass into equal parts and arrange around the inside edge of each dish. Add 2 lime leaves to each dish. Divide the leeks into neat bundles and place on top of each fillet. Cover and tightly seal each baking dish with parchment paper or aluminum foil.

Preheat the oven to 425°F. Place each baking dish on top of the stove over high heat for 1 minute, then place them in the preheated oven for 20 minutes. Remove the pans from the oven and set aside, still covered, for 4 minutes.

Mix the parsley and lemon zest in a small dish. Divide it into equal parts. Quickly open each dish and toss the mixture into the broth. Then place about $2\frac{1}{2}$ tablespoons of the seaweed salad in each pan, well to the side of the fish. Replace the cover on each dish and put on top of the stove over high heat for 1 minute.

To serve, line each of 6 large serving plates with a napkin. Place the hot dishes on the napkins, and serve immediately. Serves 6.

FRIED SHARPIES & CHORIZO CHEESE GRITS

FRIED SHARPIES

It is said that people in Florida fish more than in any other state and that no one has to travel more than ten miles to find a fishing spot. Sharpies are little catfish that are about 6 to 8 inches long. They are cooked whole, without the head. South Florida's Lake Ockeechobee is a major source of sharpies. If you can't find sharpies, use regular-size filleted catfish. When cooking, be sure not to crowd them in the pan. Serve the sharpies with hot Chorizo Cheese Grits for a good casual meal.

> $1^1/_2$ **pounds sharpies, cleaned, with heads re-**
> **moved, or 1 pound catfish fillets cut into 1-**
> **inch strips**
> **1 cup milk**
> $^3/_4$ **cup yellow cornmeal**
> $^3/_4$ **cup all-purpose flour**
> **2 teaspoons salt**
> **1 teaspoon freshly ground black pepper**
> **1 teaspoon cayenne**
> $^1/_2$ **teaspoon paprika**
> **Vegetable oil for frying**

Rinse the sharpies thoroughly and pat them dry. Place them in a bowl and cover with milk. In another bowl, combine the cornmeal, all-purpose flour, salt, peppers, and paprika. Heat about 2 inches of oil in a heavy frying pan over medium heat. Remove the catfish from the milk and dredge in the cornmeal mixture, shaking off the excess. Pan-fry until golden brown on both sides, 4 to 5 minutes. Remove and drain on paper towels.

CHORIZO CHEESE GRITS

> **1 cup uncooked regular grits**
> **1 chorizo sausage link (about 3 ounces)**
> $^2/_3$ **cup diced red bell pepper**
> $^3/_4$ **cup diced onion**
> **2 garlic cloves, minced**
> $^3/_4$ **cup shredded sharp Cheddar cheese**
> $^1/_2$ **teaspoon chopped cilantro**
> $^1/_4$ **teaspoon black pepper**
> $^1/_4$ **teaspoon ground cumin**
> $^1/_4$ **teaspoon Tabasco (or other hot sauce)**
> **3 tablespoons butter**

Cook the grits according to package directions. When done, set aside and keep warm. Remove the casing from the chorizo and discard. Place the sausage in a nonstick skillet and cook for 5 minutes over medium heat, using a fork to break apart the meat. Add the bell pepper, onion, and garlic to the skillet and continue cooking until tender, about 10 minutes. Add the sausage and vegetable mixture to the cooked grits. Add the remaining ingredients, mixing well. Pour the mixture into a 2-quart casserole and bake, uncovered, in a preheated 350°F oven for 20 minutes.

Remove the grits from the oven and allow to cool for 5 minutes to thicken before serving. Serves 4.

MUSHROOM-DUSTED SNAPPER

Allen Susser, Chef Allen's

This red snapper is enhanced by the depth of flavors of a variety of wild mushrooms and the mushroom dust, which is made from dry mushrooms, available in many supermarkets and in Asian specialty markets.

- 4 (6-ounce) red snapper fillets
- 3 tablespoons mushroom dust (see Helpful hint)
- 1½ teaspoons coarse salt
- 1 teaspoon freshly ground black pepper
- 3 tablespoons olive oil
- 2 tablespoons diced shallots
- 2 cups sliced wild mushrooms (shiitakes, oysters, chanterelles or portobellos)
- ½ teaspoon minced garlic
- ½ cup Pinot Noir wine
- ½ cup fish stock or clam broth
- 1 tablespoon chopped chives

Clean, skin, and remove any bones from the snapper fillets. In a shallow dish, combine the mushroom dust, ½ teaspoon of the salt and ¼ teaspoon of the pepper. Dredge the snapper in the mushroom mixture, lightly coating both sides.

Warm 2 tablespoons of the olive oil in a large sauté pan over medium heat. Sauté the snapper for 2 minutes, until well browned. Turn the fish over and sauté for 2 more minutes. Remove the fish to a warm oversized platter.

Add the remaining 1 tablespoon oil to the pan. Sauté the shallots over medium heat until translucent but not browned. Add the mushrooms and sauté for another 2 minutes Add the garlic, wine and fish stock. Increase the heat to high and cook for 3 to 4 minutes, until the liquid has reduced by half. Adjust the seasoning with the remaining salt and pepper and add the chives.

To serve, pour the mushrooms around the fish on the platter. Makes 4 servings.

Helpful hint: To prepare mushroom dust, buy a 6-ounce package of dried mushrooms and pulverize to a dust in a food processor fitted with a steel blade. The mushrooms will have a texture similar to coarse cornmeal. Any extra mushroom dust can be saved for another use. Serves 4.

YELLOWTAIL SNAPPER & CORN-ZUCCHINI SALSA

Paul Gjertson, Deering Bay Yacht & Country Club

Yellowtail snapper is a delicious white-fleshed fish distinguished by a broad yellow stripe from snout to tail. Particularly abundant in the Keys, it's a delicate fish, so be sure to use subtle seasonings and don't overcook it. Here it is served with a salsa, yogurt sauce and fried sweet potatoes. For a professional touch, squirt the yogurt sauce from a squeeze bottle in a zigzag pattern over the fish before serving.

Salsa
    1 medium red onion, finely chopped
    1 tablespoon sugar
    1 cup red wine vinegar
    Salt and pepper
    1 medium zucchini, green part only, diced
    2 ears fresh corn, roasted and kernels removed
    1 tablespoon olive oil

Yogurt Sauce
    1 tablespoon chopped cilantro
    1 cup nonfat yogurt
    1 teaspoon fresh lime juice
    $\frac{1}{2}$ habanero or Scotch bonnet pepper, seeded

Sweet Potatoes
    1 sweet potato, peeled and julienned
    4 cups canola oil

Yellowtail Snapper
    1 tablespoon butter
    4 (6-ounce) yellowtail fillets, with skin on
    Salt and pepper

    1 cup white flour
    $\frac{1}{4}$ cup olive oil

To make the **salsa**, combine the onion, sugar, and vinegar, and marinate for 30 minutes. Drain off the vinegar and add the zucchini and corn. Season with salt and pepper. Heat the olive oil over medium heat in a small sauté pan and cook the salsa mixture until the squash is just done. Set aside and keep warm.

For the **yogurt sauce**, combine the ingredients in a blender and puree. Transfer to a squeeze bottle and refrigerate.

To prepare the **sweet potatoes**, heat the oil to 375°F. Add the potatoes and fry until crisp. Remove, drain on paper towels and keep warm.

To cook the **snapper**, season the fillets with salt and pepper and dredge in flour, shaking off the excess. Heat a large sauté pan over medium-high heat. Add the oil and then the butter. Sauté the fillets, skin side down, until crispy. Turn and cook the other side. It will take about 5 minutes total.

To serve, divide the salsa among 4 plates, and place a fillet on top of the salsa. Squirt yogurt sauce over the fish in a zigzag pattern, and garnish with fried sweet potatoes. Serves 4.

STEAMED FLORIDA CLAMS WITH PACIFIC SPICES

Jonathan Eismann, Pacific Time

This highly seasoned and very flavorful shellfish stew can easily be multiplied to feed a crowd.

$^1/_2$ cup Rocky Mountain (or any dry) sake
$^1/_4$ cup fresh lime juice
24 fresh lime leaves (optional)
1 tablespoon Thai red curry paste
3 tablespoons sweet Hungarian paprika
1 tablespoon curry powder
1 teaspoon dark chili powder
$^1/_2$ teaspoon salt
60 fresh clams, cleaned
3 cups peeled, seeded, and chopped fresh
   tomatoes
$^1/_2$ cup minced scallions, green parts only
6 garlic cloves, sliced extra thin
1 tablespoon chopped fresh ginger
Lime leaves on branches
1 cup cilantro leaves

In a medium-size saucepan, mix together the sake, lime juice, lime leaves, curry paste, paprika, curry powder, chili powder, and salt. Add the clams and cover. Place over high heat until the clams are opened and cooked, about 5 minutes from the sight of the first steam. Remove the clams to 4 deep serving bowls and stir the tomatoes, scallions, garlic, and ginger into the remaining hot broth. Spoon the liquid evenly over the hot clams. Garnish with lime leaves on branches and cilantro. Serves 4.

PICADILLO

Doug Shook, Louie's Backyard

This is a traditional Spanish dish that can be served in bowls topped with sour cream, or with black beans and white rice, or as a dip with tortilla chips. Those familiar with the classic American dish, Sloppy Joes, will notice the resemblance.

1 pound lean ground beef
1 tablespoon olive oil
2 garlic cloves, minced
1 cup diced onion
1 cup diced red bell pepper
1 jalapeño pepper, seeded and minced
1 (28-ounce) can plum tomatoes, chopped and juice reserved
5 tablespoons capers
5 tablespoons currants
3 tablespoons cider vinegar
3 tablespoons brown sugar
1 tablespoon chili powder
1$\frac{1}{2}$ teaspoons ground cumin
1 teaspoon ground cinnamon
1 teaspoon dried oregano
$\frac{1}{4}$ teaspoon ground cloves
$\frac{1}{4}$ cup chopped Italian parsley
$\frac{1}{4}$ cup chopped cilantro
Salt and freshly ground black pepper
Sour cream

Brown the beef in a deep sauté pan over medium-high heat, then pour into a colander to drain the fat. Add the olive oil to the pan. Reduce the heat to medium, add the garlic, onion, and peppers, and sauté until the onions are translucent. Return the beef to the pan along with the other ingredients, except the fresh herbs. Bring the mixture to a boil, reduce the heat and simmer, uncovered, for 30 minutes. The picadillo should have the consistency of a thick chili. Stir in the fresh herbs and simmer for 5 minutes longer. Add salt and pepper to taste, and sour cream to garnish. Serves 4.

BARBECUE RIBS

It's amazing how many barbecue recipes exist and how many of them are "the best." Parboiling the ribs cooks out some of the fat, shortens the grilling time and helps make the outside of the meat crisp. For many, beer is the beverage of choice to serve alongside.

  8 pounds meaty pork ribs
  2 (8-ounce) cans tomato sauce
  2 cups beef stock
  $^1/_4$ cup vinegar
  1 onion, finely chopped
  3 tablespoons Worcestershire sauce
  3 tablespoons packed brown sugar
  3 garlic cloves, minced
  2 tablespoons fresh lemon juice
  2 teaspoons dry mustard
  2 to 3 tablespoons chili powder
  1 teaspoon celery seeds
  1 teaspoon salt
  $^1/_4$ teaspoon hot pepper sauce, or to taste

Trim the ribs of any excess fat and put them into a large pot. Cover the ribs with water and bring them to a boil. Simmer, covered, for 20 minutes; then remove the ribs from the water and let them cool.

Meanwhile, combine the tomato sauce, beef stock, vinegar, onion, Worcestershire sauce, brown sugar, garlic, lemon juice, mustard, chili powder, celery seeds, and salt in a saucepan. Bring the mixture to a boil, then reduce the heat and simmer about 30 minutes.

Prepare a hot fire in a grill. Grill the ribs for about 30 minutes or until tender and nicely browned, swabbing the barbecue sauce onto the ribs with a pastry brush and turning them often. (To cook them in the oven, put the ribs on a rack in a shallow roasting pan and generously coat the meat with the barbecue sauce. Bake in the middle of a 400°F oven for 45 to 60 minutes.) Serves 8.

MONGOLIAN-SPICED VEAL CHOPS

Norman Van Aken, Norman's

Mongolian-Spiced Marinade

6 garlic cloves, minced
2 teaspoons minced fresh ginger
2 tablespoons minced shallots
2 tablespoons chopped cilantro leaves
$^1/_2$ cup sherry wine vinegar
$^1/_4$ cup hoisin sauce
$^1/_3$ cup soy sauce
$^1/_3$ cup dark sesame oil
$^1/_3$ cup plum sauce
$^1/_2$ cup Spanish style peanuts, roughly chopped
2 tablespoons hot chili oil
$^1/_3$ cup honey
$^1/_3$ cup Sriracha hot chili sauce

Tamarind Soy Spice Paint

$^1/_2$ cup chicken stock
5 tablespoons soy sauce
$^1/_4$ cup dark brown sugar
$^1/_4$ cup rice wine vinegar
2 tablespoons tamarind pulp
2 tablespoons molasses
2 tablespoons minced garlic
2 inches lemongrass, sliced
1 tablespoon orange zest
2 Scotch bonnet peppers, seeded and minced
1 tablespoon roughly chopped cilantro leaves
2 teaspoons Sriracha hot chili sauce
Cracked black pepper to taste

Salad Dressing

$^1/_3$ cup rice wine vinegar
2 tablespoons mirin

$^2/_3$ cup canola oil
1-inch piece of fresh ginger, peeled and finely minced
Cracked black pepper to taste

6 (12- to 14-ounce) veal chops, trimmed
6 Japanese eggplant
Salt and freshly ground black pepper
Olive oil
6 small handfuls baby salad greens (mesclun)

Combine the **marinade** ingredients in a nonreactive bowl and mix well. Marinate the chops for 6 to 12 hours, covered, in the refrigerator.

While the veal chops are marinating, place all of the **spice paint** ingredients in a saucepan and cook over medium heat until thick enough to coat a spoon. Strain the mixture and keep warm.

To make the **salad dressing**, combine all of the ingredients and mix well. Cover and refrigerate.

Prepare a hot fire in the grill. Slice each eggplant in a fan shape up to the tip. Sprinkle with salt and pepper. Rub with a little olive oil to flavor and to keep it from sticking to the grill. Remove the veal chops from the marinade and grill them to the desired degree of doneness. Grill the eggplant at the same time. Place the veal on a plate and the eggplant next to it. Toss the lettuces with the salad dressing and drape over the veal chops. Drizzle the spice paint over the plate. Serves 6.

GOAT AND FLORIDA LOBSTER CASSOULET

Jan Jorgensen, Soren Brendahl, Two Chefs Cooking

Goat meat and lobster may seem unusual bedfellows, but they combine well in this hearty dish. If using Maine lobster, include the meat from the claws. A ceramic cassoulet dish is ideal for baking and serving. Goat meat can be purchased from Italian, Cuban, Puerto Rican, and other specialty butcher shops, especially around Easter.

$1/2$ cup white or Great Northern beans, soaked
   in water overnight
Olive oil
$1^1/2$ pounds goat meat, cut into $3/4$-inch cubes
2 carrots, diced
3 celery ribs, diced
1 Spanish onion, diced
5 garlic cloves, finely chopped
3 bay leaves
3 rosemary stalks
3 thyme sprigs
1 cup red wine
2 cups veal stock (homemade or purchased)
Salt and freshly ground black pepper
2 ($1^1/2$-pound) Florida lobsters, blanched in
   boiling water

Drain the beans, cover with fresh water and cook for about $1^1/2$ hours or until tender, then drain.

Heat a splash of oil in a large skillet over medium-high heat. Brown the goat meat well on all sides. Remove the meat and set aside. In the same pan, sauté the carrots, celery, and onion until tender but not brown. Arrange the goat meat and vegetables in a baking dish. Add the garlic, bay leaves, fresh herbs, wine, veal stock, and cooked beans, and stir to mix. Season with salt and pepper. Cover and bake in a preheated 350°F oven for about 1 hour.

Meanwhile, remove the tail meat from the lobster, cut each tail into 3 pieces, and set aside.

Remove the cassoulet dish from the oven. Add the lobster meat, cover and bake for another 15 minutes. Serve in large soup bowls. Serves 6.

CUBAN MOJO GRILLED CHICKEN

Norman Van Aken, Norman's

Chicken breasts are marinated in spicy *mojo,* a garlicky, citrus-based Cuban sauce, and accompanied by caramelized plantains and salad.

4 chicken breasts
Mojo Marinade (page 31)

Plantains

$\frac{1}{4}$ **teaspoon salt**
1 teaspoon cracked black pepper
$\frac{1}{2}$ **teaspoon toasted and ground cumin**
$\frac{1}{4}$ **teaspoon ground cinnamon**
2 very ripe plantains, peeled and cut into
   $\frac{1}{2}$**-inch diagonal slices**
Vegetable oil for frying

Citrus Vinaigrette

$\frac{1}{4}$ **cup orange juice**
$\frac{1}{4}$ **cup canola oil**
1 teaspoon honey
1 teaspoon soy sauce
Salt and freshly cracked black pepper

Salad

1 ripe mango, peeled, pitted and cut into bite-sized cubes (1 cup)
1 ripe avocado, peeled, pitted and cut into bite-sized pieces (1 cup)
Citrus Vinaigrette (see above)
2 double handfuls baby salad greens (mesclun)
Pinch salt and pepper
$\frac{1}{2}$ **cup unsalted cashews, roasted until crisp (optional)**
4 lime wedges

Combine the chicken with the marinade. Cover and refrigerate until ready to grill. (This can be done up to 3 hours in advance.)

To prepare the **plantains**, mix together the salt, pepper, cumin, and cinnamon. Lay the plantains on your cutting board and sprinkle them with the spice mix on one side. Heat $\frac{1}{8}$ inch of oil in a frying pan over medium-high heat. Set the plantains, spice side down, in the hot oil and cook until they turn golden brown to slightly black on both sides (3 to 5 minutes). Remove and drain on paper towels. Keep warm.

Combine all of the **vinaigrette** ingredients. Cover and chill. To prepare the **salad**, combine the avocado and mango in a bowl and add about 4 tablespoons of the vinaigrette. Toss gently, cover, and chill. (This can be done up to 1 hour in advance.)

Heat a grill or broiler. Broil or grill the chicken breasts, turning from time to time, until done, 6 to 8 minutes.

To serve, place the chicken and cooked plantains on 4 serving plates. Spoon the mango and avocado in a loose circle around the chicken. Toss the lettuce with the remaining dressing. Season with salt and pepper. Mound the greens over the chicken and garnish with cashews and a wedge of lime. Serve immediately. Serves 4.

GRILLED CHICKEN & CITRUS RICE

GRILLED CHICKEN

The all-American pastime of cooking outdoors is especially popular in South Florida where it's possible to grill year-round. Since the cooking time is different for the chicken and the vegetables, thread them on different skewers. Soak bamboo skewers in water for 30 minutes so they don't burn.

$1/4$ cup tarragon vinegar
3 tablespoons lemon juice
$3/4$ cup vegetable oil
2 garlic cloves, minced
1 tablespoon dried rosemary, crushed
Salt and freshly ground black pepper
$1^1/2$ pounds boneless skinless chicken thighs, cut into $1^1/2$-inch pieces
1 onion, cut into 6 chunks
1 yellow squash, cut into $1/2$-inch rounds
1 zucchini, cut into $1/2$-inch rounds
1 green bell pepper, cut into 6 chunks
1 yellow bell pepper, cut into 6 chunks
1 red bell pepper, cut into 6 chunks
6 medium-sized mushrooms
6 cherry tomatoes

Combine the vinegar, lemon juice, and oil and mix well. Add the garlic, rosemary, and salt and pepper to taste, and blend thoroughly. Put the chicken and the vegetables in a shallow dish and pour the vinaigrette over the top, mixing well. Cover and refrigerate for 30 minutes, spooning the vinaigrette over the top and turning from time to time.

When ready to cook, heat a grill or broiler. Remove the chicken and vegetables from the marinade and thread on presoaked bamboo skewers. Grill or broil, turning frequently and basting with the marinade until done, 6 to 8 minutes for tender but still crisp vegetables, and 8 to 10 minutes for the chicken. Makes 6 servings.

CITRUS RICE

Along with tourism, citrus is the most important industry in Florida, dating back to 1565. Since citrus of some kind can be grown in every part of the state, it's only natural that it finds its way into every imaginable aspect of Florida cuisine.

1 cup water
1 cup fresh orange juice (about 3 oranges)
Zest of 1 orange
1 tablespoon butter
$1^1/2$ cups long-grain white rice
$1/4$ teaspoon salt
$1/8$ teaspoon white pepper

Combine the water, orange juice, orange zest, and butter in a 3-quart saucepan and bring to a boil. Add the rice, salt, and pepper, stirring for about 30 seconds. Reduce the heat to low, cover, and cook for 15 to 20 minutes, or until the liquid has been absorbed and the rice is tender. Serve hot. Serves 4.

PUERTO RICAN ARROZ CON POLLO

Carmen Gonzalez

This Puerto Rican version of arroz con pollo includes red beans and calabaza that are cooked separately, then spooned around the chicken and rice. Caramelized plantains make a perfect side dish.

Puerto Rican Arroz Con Pollo (top) with Carmelized Plantains (bottom; recipe, page 136)

Beans

 1 pound red beans, soaked in water overnight
 $2^1/_2$ quarts water
 2 teaspoons salt
 2 tablespoons Sofrito (page 31)
 Adobo Seasoning (page 31)
 $^1/_4$ cup tomato sauce
 1 smoked ham hock
 1 bay leaf
 $^1/_4$ pound calabaza, cut in $^1/_4$-inch dice
 1 teaspoon salt
 $1^1/_2$ teaspoons black pepper

 $^1/_4$ cup extra-virgin olive oil
 $3^1/_2$-pound broiler chicken, cut into 8 pieces, rubbed with Adobo Seasoning (page 31) and marinated for at least 45 minutes
 Sofrito (page 31)
 $^2/_3$ cup white wine
 $^1/_4$ cup tomato sauce
 2 bay leaves
 3 cups chicken stock
 $2^1/_4$ cups short-grain rice
 Salt and pepper
 Caramelized Plantains (page 136)

To make the **beans**, combine the beans, water, and salt in a large pot. Bring to a boil. Reduce the heat, cover, and continue to simmer for 45 minutes or until the beans are soft. Drain. In a large saucepan, heat a little olive oil over medium heat and add 2 tablespoons of the sofrito. Cook for 10 minutes. Stir in the tomato sauce, ham hock, bay leaf, calabaza, beans, salt, and pepper. Add water to cover and bring to a boil. Reduce the heat to medium-low and continue cooking for 30 minutes.

While the beans are cooking, heat the oil in a large casserole over medium heat. Add the chicken and sauté until golden brown. Add the remaining sofrito and cook for 10 minutes. Add the wine, tomato sauce, bay leaves, and chicken stock and bring to a boil. Stir in the rice. Continue cooking, uncovered over high heat for 10 to 15 minutes, or until the water is absorbed. Reduce the heat to low and mix well, making sure that the rice on the bottom of the pan goes on top and the rice on top goes to the bottom. Cover the casserole and cook for another 20 to 30 minutes, stirring once more during this time.

To serve, mound the chicken and rice in the middle of a platter and surround it with the beans. Serve with Caramelized Plantains on the side. Serves 6.

STUFFED QUAIL WITH PLANTAINS

Efrain Veiga, Yuca

Corn Bread Rounds

2 cups all-purpose flour
2 cups yellow corn meal
6 tablespoons sugar
2 teaspoons baking powder
$\frac{1}{2}$ teaspoon Kosher salt
4 eggs
3 cups milk
1 cup melted butter (unsalted)
2 teaspoons vegetable oil

Stuffing

2 ripe plantains, peeled and cut into chunks
6 ounces chorizo sausage, diced
2 large shallots, minced
1 bunch (3 ounces) spinach, stems removed
Salt and pepper

Sauce

2 tablespoons vegetable oil
2 large shallots, minced
1 garlic clove, minced
3 ounces fresh black trumpet mushrooms
2 cups red wine
1 quart chicken stock

8 (4-ounce) quail, cleaned and boned
Salt and freshly ground black pepper
4 fresh rosemary sprigs
8 Corn Bread Rounds (see above)

At Yuca, this quail dish is topped with rings of onions that have been dipped in an egg-water mixture, then dusted with flour and deep fried.

For the **corn bread**, preheat the oven to 325°F. Butter a $6\frac{1}{2}$" x $10\frac{1}{2}$" sheet pan and set aside. Combine the dry ingredients in a mixing bowl and mix well.

Add the eggs one at a time, mixing after each. Add the milk, then the melted butter and oil. Pour the batter into the sheet pan and spread evenly. Bake for 25 minutes, or until golden. Remove from the oven. While warm, cut 8 4-inch rounds with a biscuit cutter.

For the **stuffing**, preheat the oven to 350°F. Mash the plantain with a fork in a small bowl, then transfer to a small oven-proof dish and roast for 10 minutes. Put in a mixing bowl and set aside. In a sauté pan, cook the chorizo for 3 minutes, add the shallots and cook for 2 minutes, then add the spinach and cook for 3 minutes. Drain the fat from the pan and add to the plantain mixture. Season with salt and pepper to taste.

Make the **sauce**. Heat the vegetable oil in a small pan over medium heat, add the shallots and garlic and sauté until translucent. Add the mushrooms and cook for 3 to 4 minutes. Add the red wine and chicken stock and boil until the sauce has reduced by half. You should have 2 cups of sauce.

Preheat the oven to 400°F. Season inside and outside the quail with salt and pepper. Stuff each quail with the plantain mixture. Tie the legs together with string and place on a sheet pan. Roast for 12 minutes. To serve, set a corn bread round on each plate and place 2 quails on each round. Surround with the sauce and garnish with rosemary. Serves 4.

ROASTED PLANTAIN COUSCOUS

Allen Susser, Chef Allen's

Plantains are eaten cooked—be they green, yellow, semi-ripe, or black-brown ripe. The flavors range from starchy and potato-like to caramel sweet. For this recipe, I suggest using the yellow semi-ripe plantain.

- **4 medium-size yellow-brown plantains**
- **2 tablespoons olive oil**
- **3 tablespoons diced sweet onion**
- **2 cups diced calabaza or pumpkin**
- **1½ tablespoons kosher salt**
- **1 cup fresh orange juice**
- **2 cups cold water**
- **1 (15-ounce) can garbanzo beans (chickpeas), drained**
- **2 cups instant couscous**
- **¼ cup chopped scallions**
- **¼ cup chopped cilantro**
- **1½ teaspoons crushed red pepper flakes**
- **¼ teaspoon ground cinnamon**
- **2 tablespoons extra-virgin olive oil**
- **4 tablespoons sliced and toasted almonds**

To roast the plantains, preheat the oven to 350°F. Place the plantains, with the skins on, in a shallow ceramic dish and roast for 30 to 35 minutes, until very soft. Remove the dish from the oven and set aside.

To make the couscous, heat the olive oil in a saucepan over medium-high heat. Add the onion and sauté until translucent, about 5 minutes. Add the calabaza and season with salt. Add the orange juice and the cold water. Bring to a simmer and cook the calabaza for 5 minutes, until softened. Stir in the garbanzo beans. Remove one 6-ounce ladle of calabaza, beans, and broth, and reserve for garnish. Add the couscous to the remaining mixture. Remove from the heat and pour into a large nonreactive bowl, cover with plastic wrap, and set aside for 10 minutes. Remove the wrap and add the scallions, cilantro, pepper flakes, cinnamon, and olive oil. Fluff all together with 2 large forks. Cover and set aside for another 10 minutes, then fluff again when ready to serve.

Remove the skin from the plantains and cut on a bias into 2-inch pieces. Place the sliced plantains under a hot broiler for a few minutes or until the plantains are caramelized. Remove them from the broiler.

To serve, place 3 pieces of plantain on the bottom of a ring mold 3 inches wide and 2½ inches high. Fill the mold with couscous, then top with plantains arranged in a fan. Garnish with the reserved calabaza, beans and broth, and the toasted almonds. Remove the mold and repeat for the other three servings. Serves 4.

STUFFED TOMATOES WITH CURRIED SUCCOTASH

Native Americans were cooking corn and lima beans together—succotash—when early settlers arrived in this country. Succotash is most popular in the South and there are now many variations. In this version, hollowed-out tomatoes are filled with curried succotash and warmed under the broiler. Frozen corn and lima beans may be used, but as always, fresh is better.

6 large ripe tomatoes
Salt and pepper
2 tablespoons butter
2 cups baby lima beans, cooked
Kernels from 4 ears of corn (2 cups), cooked
$1/4$ cup diced red onion
1 yellow bell pepper, diced
3 tablespoons chopped scallions
4 teaspoons curry powder
$1/2$ cup half-and-half

Cut off the top (about one-sixth) of each tomato and scoop it out, leaving a shell. Discard the seeds; chop and reserve the pulp. Salt and pepper the inside of each tomato shell and set it upside down to drain for 20 minutes. Meanwhile, melt the butter in a sauté pan over moderate heat, and add the lima beans, corn, onion, and bell pepper. Sauté until the onion and peppers are tender, about 8 minutes. Add the scallions and curry powder and sauté for 2 minutes longer. Stir in the half-and-half, chopped tomato pulp, and 1 teaspoon salt. Thicken over medium heat, about 20 minutes.

Place the tomato shells in a buttered baking dish and fill them with the succotash. Broil for 4 to 5 minutes, just until tender. Serve hot. Serves 6.

GREEN BEANS & YUCA AND ONIONS

GREEN BEANS

Though tropical produce gets the most attention, green beans are a major winter crop in the farming region just south of Miami. This dish works equally well as a hot vegetable or a cold salad.

> 3 slices lean bacon, cooked crisp, drained, and crumbled
> 1 to $1\frac{1}{2}$ pounds fresh green beans, ends trimmed
> 6 tablespoons vegetable oil
> 3 tablespoons fresh lemon juice
> 1 tablespoon finely chopped shallots
> 6 to 8 cherry tomatoes, halved
> 1 tablespoon finely chopped parsley
> Salt and freshly ground black pepper

Fill a saucepan with about 1 inch of water, add the beans, cover, and bring to a boil. Cook over medium heat for 6 to 8 minutes, or until tender but still crisp.

While the beans are cooking, combine the vegetable oil, lemon juice, and shallots in a small bowl and whisk until blended. Set aside.

Add the tomatoes to the beans and heat for about 30 seconds. Drain the cooked vegetables and refresh them in ice water. Drain again and put in a serving dish.

Pour the vinaigrette over the vegetables, add the parsley and bacon and toss to mix. Season with salt and pepper to taste. Makes 4 to 6 servings.

YUCA AND ONIONS

> 1 pound yuca, peeled, cut into $1\frac{1}{2}$-inch rings, then halved
> $\frac{1}{4}$ cup olive oil
> 1 onion, coarsely chopped
> 1 garlic clove, minced
> 1 teaspoon salt
> $\frac{1}{4}$ teaspoon pepper

In a medium saucepan, combine the yuca with about 6 cups of water and bring to a boil. Cook for 30 minutes or until the yuca is tender. Be very careful not to overcook the yuca or it will fall apart.

Meanwhile, in a small saucepan, heat the oil over medium heat and sauté the onion and garlic until they are tender but not browned, about 4 minutes.

When the yuca is tender, drain the yuca and transfer to a serving bowl. Pour the oil, onion, and garlic over the top. Sprinkle with salt and pepper. Gently toss. Serve immediately. Serves 4.

SORBETS

MANGO SORBET

1$\frac{1}{2}$ cups sugar
$\frac{1}{2}$ cup water
4 ripe mangoes, peeled and cut into chunks
   (about 4 mangoes)
2 tablespoons lemon juice
Dash of kirsch

In a saucepan, combine the sugar and water and bring to a boil to make a syrup. Set aside to cool. Puree the mango chunks in a blender. Add the puree, lemon juice, and kirsch to the syrup and stir. Chill well. Pour the mixture into an ice cream maker and freeze according to the manufacturer's directions. Yields 1$\frac{1}{4}$ quarts.

TANGERINE SORBET

$\frac{1}{2}$ cup sugar
$\frac{1}{2}$ cup water
4 cups tangerine juice (about 12 tangerines)
$\frac{1}{4}$ cup Grand Marnier
$\frac{1}{4}$ cup lemon juice

In a saucepan, combine the sugar and water. Bring the mixture to a boil, then set aside to cool. Combine the remaining ingredients with the sugar mixture and stir. Chill well. Pour the mixture into an ice cream maker and freeze according to manufacturer's directions. Yields 1$\frac{1}{4}$ quarts.

(left to right) pink grapefruit, tangerine, cantaloupe, and mango sorbets

PINK GRAPEFRUIT SORBET

$\frac{2}{3}$ cup sugar
$\frac{2}{3}$ cup water
1 cup light corn syrup
4 cups pink grapefruit juice (about 4 grape-
   fruits)
2 tablespoons lemon juice

In a saucepan, combine the sugar and water. Bring the mixture to a boil, then stir in the corn syrup. Set aside to cool. Add the remaining ingredients to the sugar mixture and stir. Chill well. Pour the mixture into an ice cream maker and freeze according to manufacturer's directions. Yields 1$\frac{1}{4}$ quarts.

CANTALOUPE SORBET

1 large ripe cantaloupe
$\frac{1}{3}$ cup sugar
3 tablespoons fresh lemon juice

Cut the melon into quarters. Scoop out and discard the seeds; remove the rind and cut the flesh into chunks. Put the chunks in a blender and puree until smooth. Measure 4 cups of puree (discard any left over). Return the measured puree to the blender and add the sugar and lemon juice. Pulse quickly to blend. Transfer to a bowl. Refrigerate, covered, until chilled, about 1 hour. Freeze in an ice cream maker according to manufacturer's directions. Yields about 1$\frac{1}{4}$ quarts.

COCONUT SORBET

Claude Troisgros, Blue Door

This simple recipe yields a refreshing and surprisingly rich tasting dessert. The frozen coconut puree used in this recipe can be found in stores that specialize in Latin American or Caribbean food.

Sugar Syrup
$^3/_4$ **cup plus 3 tablespoons sugar**
1 cup water

1 (one pound) container of frozen coconut puree
$^1/_4$ **cup plus 1 tablespoon water**
$^1/_4$ **cup plus 3 tablespoons sugar syrup**
Fresh coconut flakes (optional)

For the sugar syrup, combine the sugar and the water in a small saucepan. Bring the mixture to a boil and cook for 5 minutes. Remove the saucepan from the heat and let it cool completely.

Once the syrup has cooled, combine the coconut puree with the water and syrup. Pour the mixture into an ice cream maker and freeze according to the manufacturer's instructions. Serve with fresh coconut flakes as a garnish (optional). Yields $1^1/_4$ quarts.

MANGO SOUR CREAM CAKE

Allen Susser, Chef Allen's

This tropical fruit-topped dessert doubles as an excellent cake for breakfast with coffee.

Streusel Topping and Filling

$1/3$ cup light brown sugar
2 tablespoons white sugar
1 cup walnuts or pecans
$1^1/_2$ teaspoons cinnamon
$1/2$ cup unsifted cake flour
4 tablespoons unsalted butter
$1/2$ teaspoon vanilla extract

Batter

4 egg yolks
$2/3$ cup sour cream
$1^1/_2$ teaspoons vanilla extract
2 cups sifted cake flour
1 cup white sugar
$1/2$ teaspoon baking powder
$1/2$ teaspoon baking soda
$1/4$ teaspoon salt
$3/4$ cup unsalted butter
1 cup sliced ripe mango ($1/4$-inch slices)

Preheat the oven to 350°F. Butter a 9-inch springform pan and line the bottom with parchment paper.

To prepare the streusel topping, combine the sugars, nuts, and cinnamon in a food processor, and pulse until the nuts are coarsely chopped. Reserve $3/4$ cup for the filling. To the remainder, add the flour, butter, and vanilla and pulse briefly to form a coarse, crumbly mixture for the topping. Set aside.

To make the batter, lightly combine the yolks, about $1/4$ of the sour cream, and vanilla in a mixing bowl. In a large mixing bowl, combine the dry ingredients and mix on low speed for 30 seconds to blend. Add the butter and the remaining sour cream. Mix on low speed until the dry ingredients are moistened. Increase to medium speed (high speed if using a hand mixer) and beat for $1^1/_2$ minutes. Scrape down the sides. Gradually add the egg mixture in 3 batches, beating for 20 seconds after each addition.

Reserve about $1/3$ of the batter and scrape the remainder into the prepared pan. Smooth the surface with a spatula. Sprinkle with the $1/3$ cup reserved streusel filling and top with the mango slices. Drop the remaining batter in large blobs over the fruit and spread evenly. Sprinkle with the streusel topping.

Bake for 55 to 65 minutes, or until the cake springs back when pressed in the center. Cover loosely with buttered foil after 45 minutes to prevent the cake from overbrowning. The cake should start to shrink from the sides of the pan after it is removed from the oven. Cool on a rack for 10 minutes, then loosen the sides with a small metal spatula and remove the sides of the pan. Serves 8 to 10.

Here, the sour cream cake (photo, opposite) appears with a creamy vanilla-flecked sauce.

LUSCIOUS KEY LIME PIE

This is the most famous dessert from South Florida and the Keys. There are many recipes, and some say that the taller the meringue on this rich pie, the better. Diehards insist that only a pastry crust makes it authentic; but others prefer a graham cracker crust and say it doesn't get soggy. This pie is best served cold.

Luscious Key Lime Pie (left) and Banana Cream Pie (right; recipe, page 138)

Baked Pie Shell

2 cups all-purpose flour
1¼ teaspoons salt
¾ cup shortening
6 teaspoons ice water

5 eggs, separated
1 (14-ounce) can sweetened condensed milk
⅔ cup Key lime juice
3 tablespoons sugar

For the **pie shell**, preheat the oven to 425°F. In a mixing bowl, mix together the flour and salt. Using a pastry cutter, blend the shortening and flour until the mixture resembles small peas. Sprinkle the dough with 5 tablespoons of the water and mix with a fork until the dough forms a ball. Add additional water if necessary.

On a floured surface, roll the pastry into a circle ⅛-inch thick and gently fit it into a 9-inch pie pan. Bake for 10 minutes or until golden brown. Set aside to cool.

For the **pie**, preheat the oven to 350°F.

With an electric mixer, beat the egg yolks until they are thick and pale colored. Slowly beat in the condensed milk and blend well. Add the lime juice and mix until smooth. Pour into the baked pie shell. Bake for 15 minutes, or until the filling is firm.

In a clean bowl, beat the egg whites until they form soft peaks. Gradually add the sugar and continue to beat until the meringue holds stiff peaks. Pile and swirl the meringue on top of the pie, making sure it covers the pie completely to the crust, so it won't shrink during baking. Bake for 5 to 7 minutes, or until the meringue is light golden brown. Cool to room temperature and chill before serving. Serves 6 to 8.

COCONUT CAKE WITH KEY LIME CURD

If you like coconut, this light, fluffy, decadent dessert is for you. The tall, luscious, three-layer cake makes a handsome centerpiece and is a Southern Christmas tradition.

2½ cups all-purpose flour
1 tablespoon baking powder
½ teaspoon salt
1 cup butter, softened
2 cups sugar
4 eggs, separated
1 cup coconut milk
Seven-Minute Frosting (page 31)
Shredded coconut

Key Lime Curd
½ cup butter
1¼ cups sugar
½ cup Key lime juice
1 teaspoon grated lime zest
6 egg yolks

Preheat the oven to 350°F. Grease and flour 3 round 9-inch cake pans.

Sift together the flour, baking powder, and salt and set aside. Cream the butter and sugar in a mixing bowl until light and creamy. Add the egg yolks, one at a time, beating well after each addition. Add the dry ingredients in thirds, alternating with the coconut milk, beginning with the flour mixture.

In another bowl, beat the egg whites until stiff and glossy. Gently fold the egg whites into the batter with a spatula until well incorporated. Do not overmix. Pour the batter into the cake pans.

Bake for about 25 minutes or until the surface springs back when lightly pressed in the center, and a toothpick inserted into the middle of a layer comes out clean. Cool the cooked layers on racks for about 10 minutes, then remove from the pans and cool completely.

Meanwhile, make the **curd**. Combine the butter, sugar, and lime juice in a medium saucepan. Cook over medium heat until the sugar has dissolved. Add the lime zest and the egg yolks, one at a time, whisking constantly. Do not allow to boil. Continue to whisk until the mixture is thick and smooth, about 15 minutes. Remove from the heat and chill the curd before using.

To assemble, spread the lime curd between the layers, then frost the sides and top of the cake with the frosting. Gently press a generous amount of grated coconut into the frosting on the sides and top of the cake. Yields 12 to 16 slices.

KEY LIME SOUFFLE WITH KUMQUAT GLAZE

Christophe Gerard, Twelve Twenty, The Tides Hotel

This is an impressive dessert for special occasions. Part of its success is that it's stabilized with gelatin and cornstarch and doesn't collapse when taken from the oven. It needs to be prepared in advance since it is frozen before being cooked. The recipe doesn't divide well, so make the entire amount and keep extras on hand.

Kumquat Confit

    6 cups sugar
    24 fresh kumquats, thinly sliced

Souffle

    10 eggs, separated
    $1/4$ cup cornstarch
    12 tablespoons granulated sugar, divided
    $1 1/2$ cups fresh key lime juice
    $1/2$ cup heavy cream
    2 $1/4$-ounce envelopes unflavored gelatin

Sugar Syrup

    $1 1/2$ cups granulated sugar

    Confectioners' sugar
    2 pints fresh raspberries

For the **kumquat confit,** combine 12 cups of water and the sugar. Bring to a boil, stirring to dissolve the sugar. Add the kumquats and cook for 10 minutes or until the kumquats are soft. Remove from the heat and set aside. Don't remove the kumquats.

In a bowl, beat the egg yolks, cornstarch, and 6 tablespoons of sugar until smooth and pale. Set aside.

In a large, heavy saucepan, bring the lime juice, heavy cream, and the other 6 tablespoons of sugar to a boil. Stir until the sugar dissolves, then add a small amount to the egg yolk mixture. Gradually add the rest, constantly whisking. Return the mixture to the saucepan and while stirring constantly, cook over low heat for about 4 minutes until thickened. Do not boil or the eggs will cook.

In a small bowl, add the gelatin to $1/4$ cup of water and stir to soften. Add the gelatin to the custard and stir to dissolve. Set aside.

For the **sugar syrup,** boil the sugar and 6 tablespoons of water until the temperature reaches 240°F.

Meanwhile, beat the egg whites until stiff. Slowly pour in the sugar syrup while beating on medium speed. Continue to beat the meringue until it is cold, then fold into the custard mixture. Pour into 4-inch ring molds. Freeze for 4 hours, or until firm.

When ready to serve, unmold onto individual oven-proof plates. Place into a preheated 400°F oven, then immediately reduce the temperature to 375°F. Cook for 14–16 minutes or until nicely browned. Remove from the oven and dust with confectioners' sugar. Spoon the kumquats, berries, and a little syrup around each souffle. Serve immediately. Serves 12.

MANGO MOUSSE

Claude Troisgros, Blue Door

This light caramelized mango mousse is served with a chilled mango, mint, and rum salad.

Mousse

1 cup peeled and cut mango (1 large mango), pureed in blender
1 ($^1/_4$-ounce) packet unflavored gelatin
4 egg yolks
$^1/_2$ cup granulated sugar
2 tablespoons all-purpose flour
$^3/_4$ cup heavy cream
2 tablespoons confectioners' sugar

Mango Salad

$^1/_4$ cup granulated sugar
$^1/_4$ cup water
2 fresh mangoes, cut into cubes
$^1/_2$ cup mango juice
Juice of 1 fresh lime
$^1/_2$ cup chopped mint leaves
2 tablespoons rum
Confectioners' sugar for dusting

To make the mousse, line six 3- or 4-ounce cups or ramekins with plastic wrap. Pour 3 tablespoons of the mango puree into a small bowl. Sprinkle the gelatin over the top to soften. In a medium bowl, beat together the egg yolks, granulated sugar, and flour on high speed until thick and pale yellow, about 2 minutes.

Meanwhile, combine the remaining mango puree, 6 tablespoons of the heavy cream and the dis-solved gelatin in a medium saucepan and bring to a simmer. Stir for 1 minute to completely dissolve the gelatin. It will have a paste-like consistency. Gradually whisk this mango mixture into the egg yolk mixture. Scrape the mixture back into the saucepan and cook over medium heat, whisking constantly and scraping the bottom and corners of the pan, until the custard is thick. Do not allow to boil. Set aside to cool.

Beat the remaining 6 tablespoons cream and con-fectioners' sugar together until soft peaks form. Gently fold into the mango mixture. Pour into the pre-pared ramekins and refrigerate for at least 3 hours.

To prepare the mango salad, make a sugar syrup by boiling together the granulated sugar and the water for 5 minutes or until the sugar is dis-solved and the mixture is syrup-like. Remove from the heat and allow the sugar syrup to cool. Add the remaining salad ingredients to the cooled sugar syrup, cover, and marinate in the refrigerator for 3 hours to chill well.

To serve, divide the mango salad among 6 salad plates. Unmold the ramekins on top of the salad. Sprinkle confectioners' sugar over the top of the mousse and caramelize with a butane torch or place under the broiler briefly. Dust confectioners' sugar over the salad and the plate to create the appear-ance of a light dusting of snow. Serves 6.

WARM CHOCOLATE CAKE WITH THREE SAUCES

Todd Weisz, Turnberry Isle Resort & Club

These remarkable cakes have only 90 calories per serving. The cakes are best served warm.

Mango Ginger Sauce

  2 mangoes, peeled and cut into small chunks
  2 teaspoons minced fresh ginger
  1 cup Riesling or other semisweet white wine
  1 cup fresh orange juice

Raspberry Sauce

  1 pint fresh raspberries
  $\frac{1}{2}$ teaspoon fresh lemon juice
  Aspartame sweetener (or sugar) to taste

Blackberry Sauce

  1 pint fresh blackberries
  $\frac{1}{2}$ teaspoon fresh lemon juice
  Aspartame sweetener (or sugar) to taste

Chocolate Cakes

  5 ounces semisweet chocolate
  3 tablespoons skim milk
  1 cup sugar
  2 tablespoons butter
  3 eggs
  1 cup all-purpose unbleached flour
  1 cup whole wheat flour
  2 teaspoons baking soda
  1 cup chilled coffee
  $\frac{1}{4}$ cup dry sherry

To make the **mango sauce**, stir together all of the ingredients in a saucepan. Bring to a boil over high heat, then reduce the heat and simmer for 10 minutes. Remove from the heat and set aside to cool. Process in a blender until smooth. For the **raspberry sauce**, puree all of the ingredients in a blender and strain. For the **blackberry sauce**, repeat the same procedure as for the raspberries.

To prepare the **chocolate cakes**, preheat the oven to 350° F. Spray 4-ounce nonstick muffin tins or small brioche molds with vegetable spray. Place the chocolate, milk, sugar, and butter in a stainless steel bowl and set in a double boiler over simmering water. Stir until smooth. Remove from the heat. Slightly whip the eggs and fold them into the mixture. In a mixing bowl, combine the flours and baking soda. In another bowl, mix together the coffee and sherry. Alternate adding batches of the flour mixture and the coffee mixture to the chocolate, beginning and ending with the dry ingredients. Mix well after each addition. Spoon $\frac{1}{4}$ cup of the batter into each mold and bake for 20 minutes. Remove from the oven and turn the cakes out onto a rack.

For a dramatic presentation, spoon about 1 tablespoon of mango sauce in the middle of each plate. Drizzle a 1-inch circle of raspberry sauce around the mango sauce. Drizzle a 1-inch ring of blackberry sauce outside the raspberry sauce. Holding the plate with both hands, tap the plate on a counter, then swirl the sauce twice in a circular motion. Finally, place a cake on each plate, slightly off-center. Serve at once. Yields 16 slices.

CHOCOLATE AND PRALINE CROUSILLANT

Pascal Oudin, Sweet Donna's Country Store Restaurant & Bakery

Hazelnut Biscuit

5 egg whites
$\frac{1}{4}$ cup plus 2 tablespoons confectioners' sugar
$\frac{1}{2}$ cup hazelnut flour

Chocolate Ganache Coating

$\frac{3}{4}$ cup heavy cream
$6\frac{1}{2}$ ounces bittersweet chocolate pieces

Crousillant

1 ounce bittersweet chocolate
$\frac{1}{2}$ cup praline paste or creamy peanut butter
$\frac{1}{4}$ cup crispy rice cereal

Profiterole Sauce

$\frac{1}{2}$ cup granulated sugar
$\frac{1}{4}$ cup cocoa powder
$\frac{1}{4}$ cup water
$\frac{1}{4}$ cup heavy cream
$1\frac{1}{4}$ cup lightly whipped cream

White Chocolate Ganache

16 ounces white chocolate, in small pieces
2 cups heavy cream
$\frac{1}{2}$ cup light rum

In a mixing bowl, beat the egg whites on high speed until they hold firm peaks. Gradually add the sugar and continue to mix. Fold in the hazelnut flour, and pour onto a baking sheet lined with wax paper, spreading to $\frac{1}{4}$-inch thickness. Bake in a preheated 150°F oven for about 8 minutes. Remove and let cool. The biscuits will not be cooked firm.

For the **chocolate ganache coating**, bring the heavy cream to a boil in a small saucepan. Add the chocolate pieces, stirring to melt. Remove from the heat. Divide the ganache into two bowls, and cool.

For the **crousillant**, melt the chocolate in a small saucepan. Add the praline paste and rice cereal and mix well. Set aside.

For the **profiterole sauce**, mix the sugar and cocoa in a small saucepan. Add the water and heavy cream. Bring to a boil while stirring. Add this sauce to one portion of ganache, then add the whipped cream to the mixture.

With a $1\frac{1}{2}$-inch round cookie cutter, cut twelve circles in the hazelnut biscuit. Carefully remove them by peeling the wax paper from the bottom. Arrange $\frac{1}{2}$-inch-high mold rings on a cold baking sheet. Place each biscuit inside a ring, covering with a thin layer of crousillant mix. Fill each ring with profiterole sauce, then place the molds in the freezer for several hours, or until they are very cold.

For the **white chocolate ganache**, put the white chocolate in a bowl. Bring the cream to boil and pour it over the chocolate, stirring to melt. Add the rum.

To serve, slowly reheat the remaining portion of dark chocolate ganache. Unmold the croustillants onto a rack with a plate underneath. Pour some warm dark chocolate ganache over each. Then pour several tablespoons of warm white ganache onto each plate, placing a crousillant on top. Serves 12.

TROPICAL COOLERS

The heat and humidity in South Florida creates a nearly unquenchable thirst. Iced tea and colas are guzzled to the point of obsession, and exotic concoctions like these are cool and refreshing.

FROZEN MANGORITA

1 ripe mango
2 ounces tequila
2 ounces Triple Sec
Juice of $\frac{1}{2}$ lime
1 teaspoon sugar
Cracked ice

Peel and pit the mango, and cut it into chunks. Combine all of the ingredients, except the ice, in a blender and blend until smooth. Add up to 2 cups of ice and blend until it is finely crushed. Pour into 2 chilled margarita glasses. Yields 2 drinks.

PINEAPPLE DAIQUIRI

$\frac{1}{2}$ cup pineapple juice
2 ounces light rum
1 tablespoon lime juice
$\frac{1}{2}$ teaspoon Cointreau
$\frac{1}{2}$ cup crushed ice
Superfine sugar (optional)

Combine all of the ingredients, except the sugar, in a blender and process until smooth. Add a little sugar, if needed. Serve over ice cubes in a chilled 8- to 10-ounce old-fashioned glass. Yields 1 drink.

COSMOPOLITAN

1 ounce vodka
$\frac{1}{2}$ ounce Triple Sec
$\frac{1}{2}$ ounce Rose's Lime Juice
$\frac{3}{4}$ ounce cranberry juice
Cracked ice

Pour all of the ingredients into a cocktail shaker. Shake until the shaker feels very cold, then strain the mixture into a cocktail glass. Yields 1 drink.

ASTOR MARTINI

2 ounces orange-flavored vodka
$\frac{1}{2}$ ounce Campari
2 ounces orange juice
Cracked ice
Garnish: Slice of orange

Shake the vodka, Campari, and orange juice with the cracked ice until the shaker feels very cold. Strain the mixture into a cocktail glass and garnish with the slice of orange. Yields 1 drink.

MOJITO

$1\frac{1}{4}$ ounces dark rum
Juice of $\frac{1}{2}$ lime
2 teaspoons sugar
5 mint leaves
Ice cubes
Club soda

Combine the rum, lime juice, sugar, and mint in a blender. Blend until the mint leaves are finely minced. Pour into a highball glass partially filled with ice cubes and top off with club soda. Yields 1 drink.

RUM RUNNER

1 cup ice
3 ounces orange juice
1 ounce Captain Morgan spiced rum
$\frac{1}{2}$ ounce blackberry liqueur
$\frac{1}{2}$ ounce crème de banana liqueur
$\frac{1}{2}$ ounce grenadine

Combine all of the ingredients in a blender and process until slushy. Serve in a highball glass or other tall glass. Yields 1 drink.

LAZY LESLIE

Ice cubes
$1\frac{1}{2}$ ounces Malibu coconut rum (or other coconut rum)
1 ounce coconut milk
1 ounce grenadine
Pineapple juice

Fill a highball glass with ice cubes. Add the rum, coconut milk, and grenadine. Fill the rest of the glass with pineapple juice and stir. Yields 1 drink.

BLUE MARLIN

2 ounces light rum
1¹⁄₂ ounces blue curacao
2 ounces prepared Sour
    or Sweet and Sour Mix

Shake the rum, blue curaçao, and Sour Mix well with ice and strain into a martini glass. Yields 1 drink.

SHABEEN PUNCH

³⁄₄ ounce light rum
³⁄₄ ounce dark rum
¹⁄₂ ounce Triple Sec
¹⁄₄ cup mango juice
¹⁄₄ papaya juice
¹⁄₄ guava juice
¹⁄₄ passion fruit juice

For an 8-ounce highball glass, fill with ice cubes, and add the light rum, dark rum and Triple Sec. Fill the rest of the glass with equal parts of mango, papaya, guava and passion fruit juices and stir. Yields 1 drink.

CHOCOLATE MARTINI

Cocoa powder
1¹⁄₂ ounces vanilla vodka, chilled
1¹⁄₂ ounces white crème de cacao
1 chocolate Hershey's Kiss
Godiva chocolate liqueur

Moisten the outside of a chilled martini glass with water, then dip the rim in cocoa powder. In a cocktail shaker, combine the vodka and crème de cacao, shake well and pour into the martini glass. Drop a Hershey's Kiss into the glass and top with a dash of chocolate liqueur. Yields 1 drink.

Adapted by Scott Szabo, The Tides Hotel

Additional Recipes

CARAMELIZED PLANTAINS

Carmen González

2 tablespoons butter
2 ripe plantains, peeled and cut into 1$\frac{1}{4}$- inch rounds
1 cup light brown sugar
2 cinnamon sticks
1$\frac{1}{2}$ cups water

Heat the butter in a small saucepan over medium heat. Add the plantains and brown on both sides. Add the sugar, cinnamon sticks and water. Cook for 20 minutes or until the plantains are soft. Drain the plantains, reserving the liquid, and transfer to a serving bowl. Return the liquid to the saucepan and bring to a boil. Reduce the heat and let it cook until the liquid thickens and acquires a caramel texture.

POTATO CRACKER

Johnny Vinczencz, Astor Place, Johnny V's Kitchen

3 large baking potatoes, peeled
Vegetable oil
Salt and pepper to taste

Shred the potatoes into a bowl of water. Coat the bottom of a large sauté pan with oil and heat over medium-high heat. Squeeze the water out of the potatoes and pat dry. Sprinkle them evenly in the pan to form a thin layer and cook until brown, 7 to 8 minutes. Sprinkle with salt and pepper. Turn and cook the other side until brown and crisp. Remove from the pan and drain on paper towels. While still warm, cut into triangles about 6 inches long.

YUCA CUBES

Pascal Oudin, Sweet Donna's
Country Store Restaurant & Bakery

1 medium yuca, peeled
Grapeseed or vegetable oil for deep frying

Let the peeled yuca soak in cold water until ready to cook. Heat the oil to 350˚F in a deep-fat fryer or large, heavy saucepan. Using a vegetable peeler, shave the yuca into the hot oil in small batches so the pieces do not stick together. Cook until crisp. Drain well, then blot on paper towel.

POTATO LATKES

Johnny Vinczencz, Astor Place, Johnny V's Kitchen

4 potatoes, peeled and shredded
$\frac{1}{2}$ cup half-and half
2 eggs
$\frac{1}{2}$ cup shredded Parmesan cheese
$\frac{1}{2}$ cup bread crumbs
3 tablespoons vegetable oil
2 tablespoons sour cream
1 tablespoon chopped chives

Mix the potatoes, half-and-half, eggs, cheese and bread crumbs in a mixing bowl. Heat the oil in a nonstick omelet pan on high heat. Pour about a cup of the potato mixture into the pan. Cook until brown on the bottom, about 5 minutes, then turn and brown on the other side, about 5 minutes, or until the potato is cooked. Remove and cut into wedges. Garnish with a small dollop of sour cream and a sprig of chive.

JAMAICAN-SPICED GRILLED PORK

Mark Militello, Mark's Las Olas

6 (6- to 8-ounce) portions pork tenderloin, trimmed

Jamaican Spice Marinade

1 whole nutmeg
1 tablespoon allspice berries
1 cinnamon stick
1$^1/_2$ cups chopped onions
1$^1/_2$ cups chopped scallions
1 cup olive oil
1 cup sour orange juice
$^1/_2$ cup soy sauce
$^1/_4$ cup fresh thyme leaves
2 scotch bonnet peppers
1 tablespoon minced fresh ginger
Salt and freshly ground black pepper

For the marinade, combine the nutmeg, allspice berries and cinnamon stick in a dry skillet and toast until fragrant over low heat. Grind the spices to a fine powder in a spice mill. Combine with the remaining ingredients in a food processor and grind to a smooth paste. If desired, reserve $^1/_4$ cup for a dipping sauce or for brushing on the meat while cooking. Put the meat and the marinade in a nonreactive bowl, cover and refrigerate for several hours.

Prepare a hot fire in a grill. Grill the pork, turning often until cooked to taste, about 10 minutes. The internal temperature should register at least 150°F. Let the meat rest for 10 minutes before slicing. Serves 6.

BANANA CREAM PIE

3 cups milk
1 vanilla bean
$^3/_4$ cup cornstarch
1 tablespoon butter
$^3/_4$ cup sugar
$^1/_2$ teaspoon salt
4 egg yolks
1 baked 9-inch pie shell (page 000)
3 bananas, sliced in $^1/_4$-inch rounds

Cream Topping

1 cup heavy cream
2 teaspoons sugar
$^1/_4$ teaspoon vanilla extract

For the filling, pour 2 cups of the milk into a saucepan. Slice the vanilla bean in half lengthwise, scrape the seeds from the pod, and add the vanilla bean and seeds to the saucepan. Boil over medium-high heat for 10 minutes. Remove from the heat and take out the vanilla bean. Meanwhile, slowly mix the cornstarch into the remaining 1 cup milk. Slowly add the mixture to the cooked milk, whisking constantly. Whisk in the butter, sugar and salt. Over medium heat and add the yolks, one at a time, whisking after each. Do not allow to boil. Continue whisking until the mixture has thickened and has no lumps.

To assemble, pour one-third of the filling into the baked pie shell and cover with a layer of bananas. Add another third of the filling, then the rest of the bananas and top with the remaining filling. Just before serving, mix together the cream, sugar and vanilla in a chilled stainless steel bowl. With an electric mixer, beat on high speed until stiff. Top the pie with the cream. Serves 6 to 8.

Acknowledgments

Contributors

Jonathan Eismann, the chef/proprietor of Pacific Time, cooks Asian-influenced American food that has a French sensibility. Eismann, a graduate of the Culinary Institute of America, was given the Robert Mondavi Award for Culinary Excellence in 1994 and is featured in the Discovery Channel series, *Great Chefs of the South*.

At The Tides Hotel, **Chef Christophe Gerard** has combined traditional French techniques with the distinctive ingredients South Florida offers. At the Tide's Twelve-Twenty restaurant and at the terrace café, Gerard inspires diners with his expertise, using the best fresh fish, vegetables, fruits and spices, giving them a Mediterranean touch.

Chef **Paul Gjertson** of the Deering Bay Yacht & Country Club has lived in South Florida for the past twenty-four years. He is a graduate of Florida International University, School of Hospitality Management and worked his way through he ranks from line cook, to sous chef, to Chef de Partie.

Chef **Carmen Gonzalez** is the former chef/proprietor of the critically acclaimed Clowns restaurant in Coral Gables, Florida. She graduated with a degree in culinary arts from the New York Restaurant School in 1986. In 1995, Gonzalez founded The Feeding the Mind Foundation, a scholarship program for battered women. The foundation provides two-year scholarships to Johnson & Wales University for women from Dade County's shelters.

Cindy Hutson, chef of Norma's On the Beach, taught herself to cook as a teenager by watching *The Galloping Gourmet* and other cooking shows. She developed her New World Caribbean Cuisine by experimenting with lighter versions of traditional Caribbean dishes when she was living in Jamaica.

Jan Jorgensen and **Soren Brendahl's** restaurant, Two Chefs Cooking, began as a cooking school and cook shop but expanded in response to student incouragement. The restaurant was named the Best New Restaurant in Miami in 1997 and Best Cooking School 1994–1998 by *New Times Magazine* and one of the Best of South Florida in 1997 by *South Florida*.

Mark Militello opened Mark's Las Olas in 1994. The dishes on the menu are a refreshing combination of Caribbean ingredients and Mediterranean techniques. Mr. Militello was named one of the 10 best new chefs in America by *Food & Wine* in 1990, one of the best of the year by *Bon Appetit* in 1995, seafood chef of the year by Simply Seafood and was given the *Golden Spoon Award* by Florida Trend in 1997.

Chef Pascal Oudin was selected by *Food & Wine* as one of America's best new chefs in 1995 and by *Esquire's* restaurant critic, John Mariani, as one of America's new chefs to watch in 1995 while director and executive chef of the Grand Café at the Bay Hotel. Mr. Oudin has opened a new family-style dining concept, Sweet Donna's Country Store Restaurant & Bakery.

Chef Doug Shook discovered his love of cooking in the California wine country in the early eighties. Since 1985 he has indulged his passion at Louie's Backyard, one of few restaurant kitchens in the world with an ocean view.

Chef Dawn Sieber, a graduate of the Baltimore International Culinary Arts Institute, came to Cheeca Lodge as executive sous chef and was promoted to executive chef. At Cheeca Lodge, Sieber has created menus that blend traditional Florida Keys recipes with her own style of "new American" cuisine. Sieber has appeared on the *CBS This Morning Show* and, more recently, on the TV Food Network's *In Food Today* show.

Chef Allen Susser opened Chef Allen's in 1986, adapting his training from the New York City Technical College, School of Restaurant Management, and the Florida International University, to the the bounty of South Florida's ingredients, creating New World Cuisine. At his restaurant, Susser continues to develop this cuisine, which combines regional cultural influences and the flavors of the Caribbean. Chef Susser's restaurant has won praise from local and national food writers and the James Beard Foundation awarded him the Best Chef in America in 1994 for the Southeast Region. He is the author of *New World Cuisine and Cookery,* and his most recent book, *The Great Citrus Book.*.

Executive Chef Claude Troisgros brings his imaginative and modern French-based cuisine to the Blue Door at the Delano Hotel. Chef Troisgros, the son of a celebrated chef and restaurateur, was trained in France and spent almost twenty years in Brazil. Troisgros divides his time between Miami and Rio.

Chef Norman Van Aken is the owner of the award-winning Norman's in historic Coral Gables section of Miami. The New York Times called Norman's "the best restaurant in South Florida." Chef Van Aken is considered the "Father of New World Cuisine" and has been the recipient of two James Beard Awards, The Robert Mondavi Award, GQ's Golden Dish and The Food Arts Silver Spoon. Van Aken is the author of four cookbooks, including the Julia Child/IACP nominated *Norman's New World Cuisine.*

Chef Efrain Veiga opened Yuca in Coral Gables in 1989. Yuca (which stands for Young Upscale Cuban American) was one of the first restaurants in Florida to feature the ingredients of basic Cuban cooking in innovative, non-traditional ways, elevating the cuisine to a level it had not seen before.

Chef Johnny Vinczencz presides over Astor Place, at the Hotel Astor in Miami Beach and Johhny V's Kitchen in South Beach. After working in banquets, catering, and as chef of a popular Southwestern restaurant in Atlanta, Vinczencz relocated to South Florida and worked at several other area restaurants before becoming chef at Astor Place.

Todd Weisz is executive chef at Turnberry Isle Resort & Club, overseeing the resort's five restaurants and six kitchens. Chef Weisz ensures that only the freshest ingredients used, including produce grown in the resort's garden or native Miami and the Caribbean.

Caroline Stuart's food prepared by **Allen Smith** and **Glen Wilkes**.

Sources

Cover and page 3: flamingo from Pink Palm Company

Endpaper: painting by Matthew Popielarz, couresy of Crown Art Gallery, Inc.

Page 10: platter, salt & pepper-shaker from World Resources, pepper mill from The 24 Collection

Page 15: *South Beach*, mixed media, by Alexander Chen, courtesy of Gallery Art. © Alexander's World. Tel: (800) 332-4278

Page 24: props courtesy of The

Marlin Hotel, Arango, and Pier 1.

Page 30: platter and tray from Arango

Page 35: green plate from Helium.

Page 39: platter by Rose Gispert-Qintana, Clayworks.

Page 41: charger from Details, cutlery and salt & pepper shakers from Arango, glass from Belvetro

Page 43: plate and cutlery from Details

Page 45: platter from Cookworks of Santa Fe

Page 47: all items from Details.

Page 53: charger from World Resources, painting by Dayna Wolfe from Daynart

Page 55: soup plate/bowl from Clayworks.

Page 59: bowl and platter by Amadeo Gabino from Arango

Page 61: plates and painting by Dayna Wolfe of Daynart

Page 63: plate from Daynart, bowl from Dish, coconut wood spoon with silver bowl from Neiman Marcus, coconut wood table from The South Beach Design Group

Page 65: all props from Cookworks of Santa Fe

Page 75: table setting from Neiman Marcus.

Page 79: platter and cutlery from Arango, napkin from Details.

Page 81: cutlery from Details

Page 87: cutlery from Arango

Page 93: bowl from Helium

Page 95: platter from World Resources, knife from Details, col-

ored bowls, cutlery, and chairs from Pier 1.

Page 97: platter from Details

Page 99: ladle from Details

Page 101: table mat from Neiman Marcus.

Page 103: platter from World Resources, fork from Details.

Page 105: all props from Cookworks of Santa Fe.

Page 107: plates and cutlery from Neiman Marcus.

Page 109: platter, plate and spoon from Details

Page 111: plate from Daynart, fork from Arango

Page 115: platter and spoon from Arango, scoop from Details

Page 119: platter and plate from Daynart

Page 121: plate from Pier 1, fork from Arango

Page 123: platter from Details, cake cutter from Arango, pewter palm tree from The South Beach Design Group.

Page 125: spoon from Arango

Page 129: plate from World Resources, spoon from Arango

Page 131:plate and glass from Details.

Shops and Artists

24, The Twenty-Four Collection is a "must visit" emporium for everything from trendy French women's wear to Tibetan musical instruments. If it is beautiful, well designed, and not available just about anywhere, chances are it will be at 24. 744 Lincoln

Road, Miami Beach, FL 33139; tel: (305) 673-2455.

Arango is one of America's most celebrated design stores and a primary source for sophisticated contemporary furnishings and gifts. Arango was founded in 1959 and is now the oldest design store in the United States. Its collection includes contemporary furniture, lighting, tableware, office accessories, toys, jewelry and books. The store also holds in-store exhibitions and one-person shows., 7519 Dadeland Mall, Miami, FL 33156; tel: (305) 661-4229. www.arango-design.com.

Belvetro Glass Gallery shows all types of glass art for the occasional and serious collector. It represents over forty of the world's top glass artists, including Shane Fero, Marc Petrovic, Lino Tagliapietra and more. 934 Lincoln Road, Miami Beach, FL 33139; tel: (305) 673-6677.

Clayworks Gallery specializes in one-of-a-kind ceramics and mosaics. Most of the works are made by Rose Gispert-Qintana and Rochelle Relyea, owners of the Gallery. Rose Gispert-Qintana, originally from Barcelona, Spain, is an accomplished artist whose work can be found at Clayworks Gallery is well as other galleries and private collections. 630 F Lincoln Road, Miami Beach, FL 33139. Tel: (305) 672-7179.

Cookworks of Santa Fe stocks a wide variety of items—from professional kitchen equipment to tabletop items and gourmet food. 9700 Collins Avenue #257, Bal Harbour, FL 87501. Tel: (305) 861-5005.

Daynart artist Dayna Wolfe presents an exciting collection of hand-painted plates and platters, as well as works on canvas. Each piece is a one-of-a-kind, functional creation, bringing color and charm to any part of your home or setting. 66 NE 40th Street, Miami, FL 33137; tel: (305) 438-9866.

Details at Home has been one of South Florida's premier shopping destination since 1989. A leader in innovative design and trend-setting style, Details truly captures the essence of Florida living now. Two convenient locations offer an array of unique home furnishings, gifts, decorative accessories, bridal registry, and design services. 1031 Lincoln Road, Miami Beach, FL 33139; tel: (305) 531-1325.

Dish is the source for the never before used vintage plates, glasses and tableware. There are items for all budgets: plates, glasses and specialty items are stacked from floor to ceiling alongside crates, wagon wheels, and barrels, all with splashes of tropical color that never lets one forget that this is South Florida. 939 Lincoln Road, Miami Beach, FL 33139; tel: (305) 532-7737.

Gallery Art is a friendly place to discover affordable and beautiful art in many media. Oil, serigraphs, prints, glass, bronzes, posters—you'll find the works of many well-known artists who are respected world-wide. Promenade Shops, 20633 Biscayne Blvd., Aventura, FL 33180; tel: (305) 932-6166.

At **Helium** you can find an exquisite collection of contemporary home accessories and gifts. 760 Ocean Drive, Miami Beach, FL 33139; tel: (305) 538-4111.

Neiman Marcus is a renowned specialty store dedicated to trend-setting fashion apparel that includes designer collections for men and women, accessories, shoes, handbags, and distinctive gifts. An experienced staff assists with shopping needs and provides excellent customer service in the Neiman Marcus tradition. Neiman Marcus Bal Harbour 9700 Collins Avenue, Bal Harbour, FL 33154; tel: (305) 865-6161.

Come in to **Pier 1 Imports** and find the things that make every home unmistakably unique—furniture, candles, decorative accessories and so much more. 1224 S Dixie Highway, Coral Gables, FL 33146 or call 1 (800) 44-PIER1.

Pink Palm Company is a card and gift store that is a different shopping experience every time. The idea here is for people to find great gifts for themselves and others that have good design and great quality, at prices that keep it fun. You can also visit them at their cyberstore, www.pinkpalm.com. 737 Lincoln Road, Miami Beach, FL 33139; Tel: (305) 538-8373

Signature Limousines & Bodyguard Services 8979 Southwest 40 Street, Miami, FL 33165; tel: (305) 717-5470, fax: (305) 551-6132.

The **South Beach Design Group** gathers its collection from all corners of the world. Their team of designers are dedicated to client service and world-class design. 701 Lincoln Road, Miami Beach, FL 33139; tel: (305) 672-8800.

World Resources features one of Florida's largest collections of furniture from Indonesia and India. Located in the Miami Design District, this unique indoor/outdoor showroom displays both antiques and authentic reproductions. Miami Design District, 56 NE 40th Street, Miami,

The publisher and author would like to thank Karen Brown, Island Outpost; Kasper Van Deurs; Regina Nuessle; Rafael Croce, Freddy Castro, Signature Limousines & Bodyguard Services; and Nancy Stern, Cookworks.

We would especially like to thank all the restaurants and their staffs who helped make this project a reality:

Louie's Backyard
Chef Doug Shook
Joseph Parker
Day Chef, Darrin Swartz
Owners, Patricia Tenney and Phillip Tenney

Cheeca Lodge
Chef Dawn Seiber
Marie Leger
Brenda Le Beau

Deering Bay Yacht & Country Club
Chef Paul Gjertson

Sweet Donna's Country Store & Bakery
Chef Pascal Oudin

Norma's On The Beach
Cindy Hutson
Norma Shirley
Chef de Cuisine, Mary K. Rohan
Manager, Rose Castro

Pacific Time
Jonathan Eismann

Yuca
Owner, Efrain Veiga

Tides Hotel
David Baldwin, general manager
Chef Christophe Gerard
1220 Bar, Scott Szabo, bartender-
Joe Flores, buyer

Marlin Hotel Bar
Eddy Martinez, bartender

Turnberry Isle Resort & Club
Executive Chef, Todd Weisz

Two Chefs Cooking
Chef Jan Jorgensen
Chef Soren Brendahl
Juan Seda, bartender
Scott Kelly, waiter

Chef Allen's
Chef Allen Susser

Mark's Las Olas
Chef Mark Militello
Dana Milhiser, pastry chef

Norman's
Chef Norman Van Aken
Pastry Chef, Sam Gottleib

Blue Door at Delano
Executive Chef Claude Troisgros
Chef Luke Rinaman
Claude Roussel, Director of Food and Beverage
Hans-Jurgen Sund, pastry
Franco Colloca, Terry Zarikin, public relations

Chef Carmen Gonzalez
Alex Paradi, Assistant

Index